JOHANNA BURKHARD

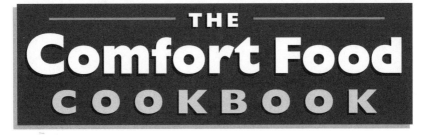

THE

Comfort Food

COOKBOOK

JOHANNA BURKHARD

THE
Comfort Food
COOKBOOK

Robert
ROSE

THE COMFORT FOOD COOKBOOK

For complete cataloguing data, see page 6.

DESIGN AND PAGE COMPOSITION:	MATTHEWS COMMUNICATIONS DESIGN
PHOTOGRAPHY:	MARK T. SHAPIRO
ART DIRECTION/FOOD PHOTOGRAPHY:	SHARON MATTHEWS
FOOD STYLIST:	KATE BUSH
PROP STYLIST:	CHARLENE ERRICSON
MANAGING EDITOR:	PETER MATTHEWS
INDEXER:	BARBARA SCHON
COLOR SCANS & FILM:	POINTONE GRAPHICS

Cover photo: OLD-FASHIONED BEEF STEW (PAGE 50)

Distributed in the U.S. by:
Firefly Books (U.S.) Inc.
P.O. Box 1338
Ellicott Station
Buffalo, NY 14205

Distributed in Canada by:
Stoddart Publishing Co. Ltd.
34 Lesmill Road
North York, Ontario
M3B 2T6

ORDER LINES
Tel: (416) 499-8412
Fax: (416) 499-8313

ORDER LINES
Tel: (416) 445-3333
Fax: (416) 445-5967

Published by: Robert Rose Inc. • 156 Duncan Mill Road, Suite 12
Toronto, Ontario, Canada M3B 2N2 Tel: (416) 449-3535

Printed in Canada

1234567 BP 00 99 98 97

CONTENTS

Canadian Cataloguing in Publication Data

Burkhard, Johanna
   The comfort food cookbook

Includes index.

ISBN 1-896503-07-1

1. Cookery.   I. Title.

TX714.B874 1997   641.5   C97-931392-9

To my family —
Nicole, Patrick and Hans
— for the many special times
we shared around the table.

Photo Prop Credit

The publisher and author wish to express their appreciation to the
following supplier of props used in the food photography appearing in
this book:

PIER 1 IMPORTS, TORONTO   DISHES, ACCESSORIES, CUTLERY, LINENS

ACKNOWLEDGMENTS

This is the book I have been longing to write for years. Now that it is a reality, I would like to thank the many people who have nurtured and nudged it along its way.

Julian Armstrong, food editor of *The Gazette*, for her unfailing support and friendship over the past ten years.

Linda Kay, my good friend and writing coach.

My kitchen assistant, Penny Kaczmarck whose help and input was invaluable.

Publisher Bob Dees for his enthusiasm and dedication to make my book idea a reality.

Sharon and Peter Matthews of Matthews Communications Design for the great design and layout of the book.

Food stylist Kate Bush and photographer Mark Shapiro for the beautiful food photos.

I am especially grateful to the many good home cooks, especially my wonderful *Gazette* readers, who have welcomed me in their kitchens, shared their family's recipes and cooking knowledge. I wish to thank them for this privilege.

I am very proud to be affiliated with the Children's Miracle Network and to have the opportunity to support and promote their worthy cause.

As a parent, I have experienced the worry and stress of having sick children. What a relief to be able to turn to a children's hospital to look after their special health needs. Through the efforts of Children's Miracle Network, we can feel secure that the high standard of care we have experienced in the past will continue despite cuts in health care.

My thanks go to *The Gazette*, *Canadian Living*, *Homemaker's* and *Elm Street*, where some of these recipes may have appeared before.

A very loving thanks to my children, Nicole and Patrick, and to my husband, Hans. They are my best food critics and their opinions have shaped so much of this book.

I'd also like to acknowledge my extended family and make a mention of my father, who relished good food. Alzheimer's recently robbed him of seeing my cookbook in print, but he would be elated to find so many of his favorite recipes.

INTRODUCTION

I remember coming home from school to the fragrant aroma of a pot roast in the oven, or maybe a smoky ham and pea soup simmering away on the back burner.

We all have our fond memories of cherished recipes that evoke the warmth of home and family. Call them our comfort foods.

Everyone has their own sense of what comfort food means. For some, it's a dish they can depend on. For others, it's ease of preparation and convenience. For still others, it's a dish that makes them feel plain good. For me, comfort food is about nurturing, with a good measure of love and caring stirred into the pot.

My goal in writing this book is not only to bring back those good memories of the past, but also to introduce some modern favorites that spell comfort for my family today. While I do include old-fashioned dishes that have never lost appeal, such as beef stew, herb-roasted chicken with garlic gravy, and cinnamon apple crumble pie, I also include new comfort foods. These have also become a staple in contemporary kitchens, and include dishes such as mushroom risotto, bistro lentils with smoked sausage, and lemon tiramisu. All these recipes share three winning characteristics: they're reliable, dependable and they taste great.

Don't feel guilty if you're not making a meal from scratch every night. I don't. There's just not enough time in our busy lives. Between our hectic schedules and the frantic pace our kids maintain, we don't need the added pressure of having to perform in the kitchen on a nightly basis. That's why many of the recipes in this book provide for next-day encores which can be reheated in the microwave oven or done ahead, so that when you do have a spare hour, you can assemble a meal and stash it away in the freezer. Once in a while, we need to slow the pace and take the time to make a leisurely meal — to tuck a pot of molasses baked beans in the oven and just sit back and enjoy the soothing aroma.

As a parent, I know that my kids' idea of comfort food includes many of the old favorites, but also embraces the fast-food tastes they're so accustomed to. I've designed a chapter specifically geared to the younger set. It contains their special comfort foods — like taco pitas, turkey fajitas, and flatbread pizzas. These recipes are simple to make and will entice kids to get in the kitchen and help with the preparation. Maybe one day, your kids will hand these recipes down to their children.

Most of the recipes in the book have been kept in line with today's guidelines for healthy eating, calling for fresh ingredients and moderate use of fat. Several of the recipes are vegetarian, inspired by my daughter's decision at the age of 15 to no longer eat meat. You'll find recipes here for black bean and corn soup, penne with oven-roasted ratatouille and stir-fried vegetables with noodles and peanut sauce. These will surely become a favorite comfort food for any vegetarian — or, for that matter, the entire family.

Nowadays, so many people don't even know the basics of cooking. The attraction of convenience products and the proliferation of quick restaurant outlets means we are spending less time in the kitchen. Even making a basic meat loaf is an event. Baking a banana bread is a lost art.

This book draws people back to the kitchen and back to basics. I chose many soul-satisfying recipes that everyone recognizes — chicken noodle soup, macaroni and cheese, date squares. These are traditional dishes that are so much a part of our food heritage and culture, yet they are recipes you rarely find grouped in one book.

I've gathered them together for you and made the directions easy to follow. *The Comfort Food Cookbook* is intended to put you at ease in the kitchen. Recipes call for ingredients that are readily available in supermarkets, so you don't have to spend hours running to specialty stores. Practical information is also given, like recipe shortcuts and other serving suggestions, to help you get dinner ready in no time.

There's no greater pleasure than the hours spent around the table sharing a meal with family and friends. The comfort foods you'll prepare from this book can be as simple as a bowl of

hearty beef and barley soup accompanied by a warm-from-the-oven slice of honey oatmeal bread, or as elaborate as a holiday meal featuring roast turkey with sage bread stuffing.

I hope to inspire you to get back in the kitchen and recreate those special memories — and establish some new food traditions with your own family.

Johanna Burkhard

AN APPRECIATION

The Children's Miracle Network (CMN) is an international non-profit organization dedicated to raising funds and awareness for children's hospitals and foundations. Founded in 1983, CMN's first fund-raising effort was a national television special broadcast by 30 TV stations and benefiting 22 hospitals. It raised $4.7 million.

In 15 years, CMN has raised over $1 billion for the cause! There are currently 11 member children's hospitals and foundations in Canada, out of a total of 165 throughout North America. These Canadian members raise an astonishing 20-25% of the total funds each year. **All funds raised in Canada stay right in the local community to benefit the hospitals, foundations and health centres serving the area where it was raised.** This has been the cornerstone of our success over the years. Consumers and corporate sponsors have the security of knowing that the funds they raise are helping children in their own neighbourhoods.

Children's hospitals in Canada treat over 2 million children each year — children like Amanda, diagnosed with leukemia at only 6 weeks old. By her third birthday Amanda required a bone marrow transplant and the perfect match was her 15-month-old sister, Becky. The transplant was a success and Amanda is now cancer-free and in perfect health. She and Becky are inseparable and as she hugs her sister, Amanda tells all their admirers, "This is my sister. She saved my life!"

Indeed, Amanda's sister did save her life — but so did the many doctors, nurses, support staff and volunteers associated with one of the finest pediatric hospitals in the world, right here in Canada. The research, technology and equipment required to fund procedures like this one — as well as the ongoing work in prevention and treatment of childhood diseases, birth defects and life threatening accidents and illnesses — are the reason CMN exists.

Funds raised through CMN programs are used by the hospitals and health centres to ensure that a high level of specialized care is available to our children when they need it and to continue outreach, wellness and safety programs to keep children healthy and happy in their communities.

The Children's Miracle Network and its affiliates across Canada sincerely thank Johanna Burkhard for her generosity in dedicating a portion of the sale of this book to the health of our children. What could be more appropriate than the word "comfort" when thinking of a child — and knowing our goal is to have them home around the table being nurtured with love and good home cooking?

On behalf of all the children who will benefit in so many ways from this project, our heartfelt thanks!

Sincerely,

Stephanie Melemis

VICE-PRESIDENT, CANADA
CHILDREN'S MIRACLE NETWORK

APPETIZERS

Creamy Mushroom-Walnut Toasts

Makes about 40

Want a great start to a meal? Begin here. I always have containers of this delicious mushroom spread in my freezer ready to defrost in the microwave when friends or family drop by. The same applies for the bread, which I slice, pack into plastic bags and freeze.

TIP

Toasted baguette slices

Cut 1 thin baguette (French bread) into 1/3-inch (8 mm) thick slices. Arrange on baking sheet; brush lightly with 2 tbsp (25 mL) olive oil. Bake in 375° F (190° C) oven for 5 minutes or until edges are lightly toasted. Spread toasts with mushroom mixture just before baking to prevent them from turning soggy.

◆

Mushroom-walnut filling can be frozen for up to 2 months.

◆

To wash or not wash mushrooms? You can wipe them with a damp cloth, if you wish. However, I feel it's important to wash all produce that comes into my kitchen. I quickly rinse mushrooms under cold water and immediately wrap in a clean, dry kitchen towel (or paper towels) to absorb excess moisture.

Preheat oven to 375° F (190° C)
Baking sheet

1 lb	mushrooms (an assortment of white, oyster and portobello), coarsely chopped	500 g
2 tbsp	butter	25 mL
1/3 cup	finely chopped green onions	75 mL
2	cloves garlic, minced	2
1/2 tsp	dried thyme	2 mL
4 oz	light cream cheese *or* goat cheese, cut into pieces	125 g
1/3 cup	freshly grated Parmesan cheese (plus extra for topping)	75 mL
1/3 cup	finely chopped walnuts	75 mL
2 tbsp	finely chopped fresh parsley	25 mL
	Salt and pepper	
40	toasted baguette slices (see Tip, at left)	40

1. Using a food processor, finely chop mushrooms in batches using on-off turns.

2. In a large skillet, heat butter over medium-high heat. Add mushrooms, onions, garlic and thyme; cook for 5 to 7 minutes or until mushrooms are softened. Cook 1 to 2 minutes more, if necessary, until all moisture has evaporated. (Mixture should be dry and almost crumbly.) Remove from heat.

3. Add cream cheese, stirring until smooth. Add Parmesan cheese, walnuts and parsley. Season with salt and pepper to taste. Transfer to a bowl; cover and let cool.

4. Spread toasted baguette slices with a generous teaspoonful (5 to 7 mL) of mushroom mixture. Arrange on baking sheet. Sprinkle tops with additional Parmesan cheese. Bake in preheated oven for 8 to 10 minutes or until edges are toasted.

Makes about 48 croustades

VARIATION
Mushroom Walnut Croustades

Instead of baguette slices, try making croustades (toasted bread cups). They are excellent for this dish and also make ideal containers for a wide range of fillings.

1. Using a serrated knife, remove crusts from 1 loaf white or whole-wheat sandwich bread. (Reserve trimmings for making stuffing and bread crumbs.) With a rolling pin, flatten each slice. Using a 2-inch (5 cm) pastry cutter, cut out bread rounds. (You will get 3 to 4 rounds per slice depending on bread size.) Press into well-buttered or oiled small muffin or tart pans. Lightly brush with 3 tbsp (45 mL) melted butter or olive oil. Bake in 375° F (190° C) oven for 10 to 12 minutes or until toasted and crisp. (Toasted rounds can be made ahead; place in containers and freeze for up to 1 month.)

2. Fill croustades with mushroom-walnut mixture; sprinkle with Parmesan cheese. Arrange on baking sheet; bake in 375° F (190° C) oven for 8 minutes or until heated through.

Creamy Spinach Dip

Makes 3 cups (750 mL)

Here's a dip that's so much tastier than the ones made with salty soup mixes. Serve with vegetable dippers such as carrot, pepper, cucumber, celery, broccoli, fennel and cauliflower. I use any leftovers as a dressing for pasta or potato salads, or as a spread for sandwiches.

TIP

To grate lemon rind, use a zester to remove the rind in thin shreds and finely chop with knife.

When lemons are bargain-priced, stock up for the future: Grate the rinds and squeeze the juice; place in separate containers and freeze.

◆

To make a bread bowl for serving: Using a serrated knife, slice 2 inches (5 cm) off top of small (1 lb [500 g]) unsliced round whole wheat or sourdough bread. Hollow out loaf, reserving contents, leaving a shell about 1 inch (2.5 cm) thick. Spoon dip into bread bowl. Cut reserved bread into strips or cubes and serve along with vegetables dippers.

1	pkg (10 oz [300 g]) fresh or frozen spinach	1
1 cup	crumbed feta cheese (about 4 oz [125 g])	250 mL
1/3 cup	chopped green onions	75 mL
1/4 cup	chopped fresh dill	50 mL
1	clove garlic, minced	1
1 tsp	grated lemon rind	5 mL
1 1/2 cups	sour cream (regular or light)	375 mL
1/2 cup	light mayonnaise	125 mL

1. Remove tough stem ends from fresh spinach; wash in cold water. Place spinach with moisture clinging to leaves in a large saucepan. Cook over high heat, stirring, until just wilted. (If using frozen spinach, remove packaging and place in a glass bowl; microwave at High, stirring twice, for 5 minutes or until completely defrosted.) Place spinach in a colander to drain. Squeeze out moisture by hand; wrap in a clean, dry towel and squeeze out excess moisture.

2. In a food processor, combine spinach, feta, onions, dill, garlic and lemon rind. Process until very finely chopped.

3. Add sour cream and mayonnaise; process, using on-off turns, just until combined. Transfer to a serving bowl, cover and refrigerate until ready to serve. Serve in a bread bowl (see Tip, at left), if desired, and accompany with vegetable dippers.

Party Pâté

Makes 2 1/2 cups (625 mL)

Here's a modern spin to an old standby, chicken liver spread. Even if you're not a big fan of liver, you'll be instantly won over when you try this lightly sweetened pâté with currants and Port. Serve with warm toasted baguette slices.

TIP

Make the pâté up to 3 days ahead. Cover surface with plastic wrap and refrigerate. Or pack into containers and freeze for up to 1 month.

◆

Like freshly ground pepper, the taste of freshly grated nutmeg is so much better than the pre-ground variety. Whole nutmeg can be found in the spice section of your supermarket or bulk food store. Look for inexpensive nutmeg graters in kitchenware shops.

3 tbsp	dried currants	45 mL
3 tbsp	ruby Port	45 mL
1 lb	chicken livers	500 g
2 tbsp	butter	25 mL
1	medium onion, finely chopped	1
1 cup	peeled, chopped apples	250 mL
3/4 tsp	salt	4 mL
1/2 tsp	rubbed sage	2 mL
1/2 tsp	pepper	2 mL
1/4 tsp	nutmeg	1 mL
1/3 cup	butter, cut into small cubes	75 mL

1. In a small glass dish, combine currants and Port; microwave at High for 1 minute until plump. Set aside.

2. Trim chicken livers and cut into quarters. Place in a large nonstick skillet with 1/2 cup (125 mL) water; bring to a boil over medium heat, stirring often, for 5 minutes or until no longer pink. Drain in sieve; transfer to bowl of food processor.

3. Rinse and dry skillet; add 2 tbsp (25 mL) of the butter and melt over medium heat. Add onion, apples, salt, sage, pepper and nutmeg; cook, stirring often, for 5 minutes or until softened.

4. Add onion-apple mixture to liver in bowl of food processor; purée until very smooth. Let cool slightly. Add butter cubes to liver mixture and purée until creamy. Add reserved currants and Port; pulse, using on-off turns, until just combined.

5. Spoon into a serving bowl. Cover surface with plastic wrap and refrigerate until firm, about 4 hours or overnight.

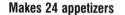

Antipasto Nibblers

Makes 24 appetizers

Here's another last-minute idea for tasty bites to serve when friends drop over. These small nibblers are a throwback to the cocktail/lounge scene of the 1960s, when appetizers often meant cold cuts wrapped around a pickle. I like them because they can be assembled in a few minutes and are a colorful addition to a tray of warm appetizers.

TIP

This recipe can be varied according to what you have on hand. Thin slices of salami or ham folded in half, cocktail onions and marinated artichoke pieces make for other easy combinations.

24	stuffed green olives *or* Kalamata olives	24
8 oz	Fontina cheese, cut into 3/4-inch (2 cm) cubes	250 g
1	small sweet red pepper, cut into 1-inch (2.5 cm) squares	1
1	small sweet green pepper, cut into 1-inch (2.5 cm) squares	1
1 tbsp	olive oil	15 mL
1 tbsp	balsamic vinegar	15 mL
	Pepper	
2 tbsp	chopped fresh basil *or* parsley	25 mL

1. Thread 1 olive, 1 cheese cube, then 1 pepper square on cocktail toothpicks. Arrange in attractive shallow serving dish. Cover and refrigerate until serving time.

2. In a small bowl, whisk together oil and balsamic vinegar; pour over kabobs. Season generously with pepper; sprinkle with basil and serve.

Nippy Parmesan Cheese Straws

Makes about 64

I make double batches of these wonderfully cheese-laden sticks, especially at holiday time. They are perfect as appetizers and great to serve along with soup. To obtain the richest flavor, buy a wedge of authentic *Parmigiano Reggiano* and have it finely grated for you at the cheese shop.

TIP

Baked straws can be stored in covered container for up to 5 days. Or freeze unbaked straws for up to 2 months in a covered container lined with waxed paper. No need to defrost before baking.

Preheat oven to 375° F (190° C)
Baking sheet(s) lined with parchment paper

1 cup	freshly grated Parmesan cheese	250 mL
1/2 tsp	sweet Hungarian paprika	2 mL
1/4 tsp	cayenne pepper	1 mL
1	pkg (1 lb [400 g]) puff pastry (2 sheets)	1

1. In a bowl combine Parmesan, paprika and cayenne pepper.

2. Sprinkle work surface with 2 tbsp (25 mL) of the Parmesan mixture to cover an area approximately the same size as 1 pastry sheet. Place pastry sheet to cover sprinkled Parmesan mixture; sprinkle top of sheet with another 2 tbsp (25 mL) of the Parmesan mixture.

3. Roll out pastry to make a 10-inch (25 cm) square. Sprinkle half the pastry with 2 tbsp (25 mL) of the Parmesan mixture; fold dough over in half. Sprinkle with 2 tbsp (25 mL) more Parmesan mixture. Roll out to make a thin 12- by 10-inch (30 by 25 cm) rectangle. Cut dough in half to make two 12- by 5-inch (30 by 12.5 cm) rectangles.

4. With a sharp knife and using a ruler as a guide, cut pastry into strips measuring 5 by 3/4 inches (13 by 2 cm); twist each strip 3 or 4 times to make a spiral. Arrange on parchment paper-lined baking sheets, pressing the ends onto the sheets to hold them in place.

5. Repeat steps 2 through 4 with second pastry sheet and remaining Parmesan mixture.

6. Freeze for 15 minutes or until pastry is firm. Bake in preheated oven for 14 to 16 minutes or until puffed and golden. Transfer to a rack to cool.

Smoked Salmon Mousse

Makes 3 cups (750 mL)

This is one of my most requested recipes. It delivers a wonderful smoked salmon flavor, but uses relatively little of that costly ingredient. My secret? I work magic with canned salmon, which keeps the cost reasonable so I can serve this appetizer more often.

TIP

I prefer to use canned sockeye salmon (instead of the pink variety) for its superior color and flavor.

◆

The mousse can be prepared up to 4 days ahead for easy entertaining.

◆

To get more juice out of a lemon, roll on counter top or microwave at High for 20 seconds before squeezing.

1/3 cup	dry white wine *or* water	75 mL
1	pkg (1/4 oz [7 g]) unflavored gelatin	1
1	can (7 1/2 oz [213 g]) sockeye salmon, drained, skin removed	1
1 cup	sour cream	250 mL
1 tbsp	fresh lemon juice	15 mL
1/2 tsp	grated lemon rind	2 mL
1/4 tsp	salt	1 mL
	Hot pepper sauce, to taste	
4 oz	smoked salmon, finely chopped	125 g
2 tbsp	minced green onions	25 mL
2 tbsp	finely chopped fresh dill	25 mL
1/2 cup	whipping (35%) cream, whipped	125 mL
	Dill sprigs and lemon zest for garnish	

1. Place wine in a small bowl; sprinkle gelatin over. Let stand 5 minutes to soften. Microwave at Medium for 1 minute or until dissolved.

2. In a food processor, combine canned salmon, sour cream, lemon juice and rind, salt and hot pepper sauce; process until smooth. Add gelatin mixture; process until combined.

3. Transfer mixture to a bowl. Stir in smoked salmon, onions and dill; fold in whipped cream.

4. Spoon mixture into serving dish. Cover loosely with plastic wrap (it should not touch surface of the mousse); refrigerate for 4 hours or overnight. Garnish top with dill sprigs and lemon zest; serve with melba toast or pumpernickel rounds.

Rosy Shrimp Spread

**Makes 1 1/4 cups
(300 mL)**

Using ingredients you keep on hand in the pantry and in the fridge, you can whip up this reliable recipe in only a few minutes. You'll turn to it, as I have, time and time again.

4 oz	light cream cheese, softened	125 g
1/4 cup	light sour cream *or* plain yogurt	50 mL
2 tbsp	prepared chili sauce	25 mL
1 tsp	prepared horseradish	5 mL
	Hot pepper sauce, to taste	
1	can (4 oz [113 g]) small shrimp, rinsed and drained	1
1 tbsp	minced green onion tops *or* chives	15 mL

1. In a bowl, beat cream cheese until smooth. Stir in sour cream, chili sauce, horseradish and hot pepper sauce.

2. Fold in shrimp and green onions. Transfer to serving dish; cover and refrigerate until serving time.

Sweet-and-Sour Meatballs

Serves 6 to 8

Who doesn't love meatballs as an appetizer? As fast as I fill the serving bowls with them, they disappear.

TIP

This versatile dipping sauce is also good with chicken or pork kebabs, or with chicken wings. For a spicy version, add hot pepper sauce to taste.

1/2 cup	orange juice	125 mL
1/4 cup	soya sauce	50 mL
1/4 cup	ketchup	50 mL
1/4 cup	brown sugar	50 mL
2 tbsp	balsamic vinegar	25 mL
1	garlic clove, minced	1
1 1/2 tsp	cornstarch	7 mL
36	appetizer meatballs (half recipe, BASIC MEATBALLS; see recipe, facing page)	36

1. In a medium saucepan, stir together orange juice, soya sauce, ketchup, brown sugar, vinegar, garlic and cornstarch until smooth. Bring to a boil over medium heat, stirring constantly, until sauce is thick and smooth.

2. Stir in cooked meatballs; cover and simmer for 5 minutes or until heated through.

Basic Meatballs

Makes about 72 appetizers
or 48 meatballs for
SPAGHETTI AND MEATBALLS
(see recipe, page 103)

TIP

Spaghetti Meatballs

Follow recipe as given but
increase size of meatballs to
1 1/2 inches (4 cm) and
lengthen baking time to
25 minutes.

♦

Take advantage of supermarket
specials and buy lean ground
beef in bulk to make batches
of these tasty meatballs.
Keep them in the freezer for
quick appetizers or to use in
pasta sauces.

♦

Cooked meatballs can be
made up to 1 day ahead
and kept covered in the
refrigerator, or frozen for up to
2 months. To freeze, place
meatballs in a single layer
on trays; when frozen, transfer
to covered containers.
To defrost quickly, place
meatballs in a casserole dish
and microwave at High for
4 to 5 minutes until just
warmed through,
stirring once.

Preheat oven to 400° F (200° C)
Rimmed baking sheet, greased

1 tbsp	vegetable oil	15 mL
1	medium onion, finely chopped	1
2	cloves garlic, minced	2
3/4 tsp	salt	4 mL
1/2 tsp	dried thyme	2 mL
1/2 tsp	pepper	2 mL
1/2 cup	beef stock	125 mL
2 tsp	Worcestershire sauce	10 mL
2 lbs	lean ground beef	1 kg
1 cup	soft bread crumbs	250 mL
2 tbsp	finely chopped fresh parsley	25 mL
1	large egg, lightly beaten	1

1. In a medium nonstick skillet, heat oil over medium heat. Add onion, garlic, salt, thyme and pepper; cook, stirring often, for 5 minutes or until softened. Stir in beef stock and Worcestershire sauce; let cool slightly.

2. In a bowl combine onion mixture, ground beef, bread crumbs, parsley and egg; mix thoroughly.

3. Form beef mixture into 1-inch (2.5 cm) balls; arrange on rimmed baking sheet. Bake in preheated oven for 18 to 20 minutes or until nicely browned. Transfer to a paper towel-lined plate to drain.

Artichoke Phyllo Triangles

Makes 48 triangles

Phyllo pastry makes great crisp wrappers for a variety of savory fillings. The pastry is used extensively in Mediterranean cooking and fits in perfectly with the modern notion of comfort foods because it delivers taste, style and convenience, too. I make batches of these Greek-inspired appetizers ahead and then freeze them. The only thing left to do is pop them in the oven and serve.

TIP

To freeze, place unbaked triangles on baking sheets; freeze until firm. Place in waxed paper-lined containers; freeze for up to 2 months. No need to defrost before baking.

◆

The artichoke filling also freezes well. Pack into containers and freeze for up to 2 months.

◆

Sun-dried tomatoes sold dry in packages are more economical than those packed in oil. To reconstitute, place in a bowl and cover with boiling water. Or cover with cold water and microwave at High for 2 minutes or until just boiling. Let stand for 10 minutes or until softened; drain and chop.

Preheat oven to 375° F (190° C)
Baking sheet, lightly greased

1 tbsp	olive oil	15 mL
1	can (14 oz [398 mL]) artichoke hearts or bottoms, drained well, finely chopped	1
4	green onions, finely chopped	4
2	cloves garlic, minced	2
1 tsp	dried oregano	5 mL
1/4 cup	finely chopped sun-dried tomatoes	50 mL
1/4 cup	finely chopped Kalamata olives	50 mL
1 cup	shredded Gruyere cheese	250 mL
1/4 cup	freshly grated Parmesan cheese, (plus extra for topping)	50 mL
	Pepper	
6	sheets phyllo pastry	6
1/3 cup	olive oil *or* melted butter (approximate)	75 mL

1. In a large nonstick skillet, heat oil over medium-high heat. Add artichokes, onions, garlic and oregano; cook, stirring, for 3 minutes or until softened. Stir in sun-dried tomatoes and olives. Remove from heat; transfer to bowl and let cool slightly.

2. Stir in Gruyere and Parmesan cheeses; season with pepper. (Recipe can be prepared up to this point, then kept covered and refrigerated, up to 3 days ahead.)

3. Place 1 phyllo sheet on work surface. (To prevent remaining sheets from drying out, keep them covered with waxed paper, then a damp kitchen towel.) Brush pastry lightly with oil or melted butter. Cut crosswise into 8 strips, each 2 inches (5 cm) wide.

VARIATION

Spread artichoke filling on lightly toasted baguette slices or spoon in croustades (see MUSHROOM-WALNUT CROUSTADES, recipe page 19); sprinkle with additional Parmesan cheese. Bake in 375° F (190° C) for 8 minutes or until heated through.

4. Place 1 tsp (5 mL) filling at bottom-left corner of each strip; fold right corner over filling to meet the left side to form a triangle. Continue wrapping pastry around filling, maintaining a triangular shape.

5. Place on prepared baking sheet. Brush top lightly with olive oil. Continue making triangles with remaining phyllo and filling in the same way. Bake in preheated oven for 14 to 16 minutes or until golden.

Warm Salsa Dip

Makes 3 cups (750 mL)

This dip will draw raves from a gang of starving teens or a crowd around the TV set when the ball game is in progress.

In our house, we usually can't agree if we want the dip hot or mild. The solution? I use mild salsa as the base and once the dip is made, divide it into 2 bowls. I leave one mild and add plenty of hot sauce or minced pickled jalapenos to spice up the other. Give the dip a quick reheat in the microwave if it cools — assuming it lasts that long, of course!

TIP

A lower-fat alternative to tortilla chips are pita crisps. To make them: Separate three 7-inch (18 cm) pita breads into rounds and cut each into 8 wedges. Place in single layer on baking sheets; bake at 350° F (180° C) for 8 to 10 minutes or until crisp and lightly toasted. Let cool. Store in covered container. The pita crisps can be made 1 day ahead.

1	can (19 oz [540 mL]) white kidney beans, drained and rinsed	1
1 cup	store-bought mild or hot salsa	250 mL
2	cloves garlic, minced	2
1 tsp	ground cumin	5 mL
1 tsp	dried oregano	5 mL
4 oz	light cream cheese, cubed and softened	125 g
1 cup	shredded mozzarella cheese *or* Monterey Jack *or* white Cheddar cheese	250 mL
	Tortilla chips *or* pita crisps	

1. In a bowl, mash beans with fork until quite smooth.

2. In a medium saucepan, combine beans, salsa, garlic, peppers, cumin and oregano. Place over medium heat, stirring often, until piping hot.

3. Stir in cream cheese; stir until dip is smooth. Add mozzarella; stir until melted. Serve warm with tortilla or pita crisps.

Microwave method:

1. Combine all the ingredients in microwaveable bowl. Microwave at Medium-High, stirring twice, for 5 to 7 minutes, or until heated through and cheese is melted. Serve warm with tortilla or pita crisps.

Cheddar Pepper Rounds

Makes about 48 rounds

Here's an updated version of the classic cheese ball, an appetizer that dominated the party scene in the 1950s and 1960s. This recipe may seem to call for a lot of peppercorns, but it's not all that peppery. It just has a lively zip.

TIP

To crack peppercorns, place in a heavy plastic bag and, on a wooden board, crush using a rolling pin or heavy skillet.

◆

Cheese logs can be frozen for up to 1 month. Defrost in the refrigerator for several hours before slicing.

VARIATION

Cheddar Walnut Rounds
Substitute 1/3 cup (75 mL) finely chopped walnuts or pecans for black peppercorns.

8 oz	aged Cheddar cheese, shredded	250 g
4 oz	light cream cheese	125 g
2 tbsp	brandy *or* sherry	25 mL
1/4 cup	finely chopped fresh parsley	50 mL
1 tbsp	cracked black peppercorns	15 mL

1. In a food processor, combine Cheddar cheese, cream cheese and brandy. Process until mixture is very smooth. Transfer to a bowl; refrigerate for 3 hours or until firm.

2. Divide mixture into 2 pieces; wrap each in plastic wrap. Roll on a flat surface and shape into a smooth log measuring about 6 inches by 1 1/2 inches (15 by 4 cm).

3. Place parsley and cracked peppercorns on a plate. Unwrap cheese logs and roll in parsley-peppercorn mixture until evenly coated. Wrap again in plastic wrap and refrigerate until firm.

4. To serve, cut each log into 1/4-inch (5 mm) slices and place on small toasted bread rounds, melba toasts or crackers.

Honey-Garlic Chicken Wings

**Serves 8 as an appetizer
or 4 as a main course**

These spicy wings are always a party hit. They're deliciously messy, so be sure to have plenty of napkins on hand.

TIP

You can also partially cook the wings in the oven for the first 20 minutes and complete the cooking on the barbecue over medium heat.

◆

Taste the marinade sauce before adding to the chicken wings; it should have a nice zip to it.

**Preheat oven to 400° F (200° C)
Rimmed baking sheet, lined with foil then brushed with oil**

3 lbs	chicken wings, separated and tips removed	1.5 kg
1/3 cup	soya sauce	75 mL
1/4 cup	honey	50 mL
2 tbsp	hoisin sauce	25 mL
2 tbsp	rice vinegar	25 mL
2	large cloves garlic, minced	2
2 tsp	hot pepper sauce, or more to taste	10 mL

1. Place chicken wings in a large heavy plastic bag and set in a large bowl. In a small bowl, combine soya sauce, honey, hoisin sauce, vinegar, garlic and hot pepper sauce. Pour over wings, close tightly and seal. Let marinate in fridge for several hours or overnight.

2. On prepared baking sheet, arrange wings in a single layer; bake in preheated oven for 20 minutes. Pour off pan juices and turn wings over.

3. Meanwhile, place marinade in a small saucepan. Bring to a boil over medium heat; cook 3 to 5 minutes or until slightly thickened. Baste wings liberally with marinade.

4. Bake 15 to 20 minutes more or until wings are tender and nicely glazed.

SMOKED SALMON MOUSSE (PAGE 24) ➤

Baked Brie with Cranberry-Pear Chutney

Serves 4

This makes a very simple but delicious appetizer. If you are expecting a large crowd, buy a larger wheel of Brie and top with generous layer of chutney and chopped walnuts. Bake a few minutes longer or until sides are soft to the touch.

TIP

Make extra batches of the chutney and pack the hot mixture into sterilized 1-cup (250 mL) preserving jars and fit with 2-piece lids. Process in boiling water bath for 10 minutes to ensure a vacuum seal.

◆

A jar of this chutney tied with a colorful swatch of fabric and a pretty ribbon makes a wonderful hostess gift.

◆

It also makes a fabulous condiment to serve with ROAST TURKEY (see recipe, page 62) or try it with QUEBEC MEAT PIE (see recipe, page 74).

Preheat oven to 350° F (180° C)
Baking sheet lined with foil

1	round of Brie cheese (7 oz [210 g])	1
1/4 cup	CRANBERRY-PEAR CHUTNEY (recipe follows)	50 mL
2 tbsp	finely chopped walnuts	25 mL
	Baguette slices	

1. Arrange Brie on prepared baking sheet. Spread top with chutney; sprinkle with walnuts.

2. Bake in preheated oven for 5 to 7 minutes or until sides of Brie are soft to the touch. Using a metal spatula, transfer to a serving plate; surround with bread slices. Serve warm.

CRANBERRY-PEAR CHUTNEY
Makes about 3 cups (750 mL)

3 cups	fresh or frozen cranberries	750 mL
1 1/2 cups	peeled finely diced pears, such as Anjou	375 mL
1	small onion, finely chopped	1
1 cup	packed brown sugar	250 mL
1/2 cup	orange juice	125 mL
1/2 cup	cider vinegar	125 mL
1/2 cup	golden raisins	125 mL
1 tbsp	grated orange rind	15 mL
1 tsp	ground ginger	5 mL

1. In a large saucepan, combine cranberries, pears, onion, brown sugar, orange juice, vinegar, raisins, orange rind and ginger. Bring to a boil over medium heat.

2. Simmer, uncovered, stirring occasionally, for 15 to 20 minutes or until mixture has thickened and fruit is tender.

◄ CHEESE-SMOTHERED ONION SOUP (PAGE 36)

SOUPS

Cheese-Smothered Onion Soup

Serves 6

A good melting cheese with a nice nutty flavor (such as Gruyere or Raclette) works very well in this savory soup which warms you up on cold blustery days.
The assertive flavor of onions mellows and sweetens when cooked until golden. This classic makes an easy transition from an everyday dish to an entertainment standout.

TIP

Buy French bread 3 to 4 inches (8 to 10 cm) in diameter. Or, if using a thin baguette, use 2 slices of bread in each bowl.

◆

The onion soup base can be made ahead and refrigerated for up to 5 days or frozen for up to 3 months.

◆

Hate shedding tears when chopping onions?
To minimize the weeping problem, use a razor-sharp knife to prevent loss of juices and cover the cut onions with a paper towel as you chop them to prevent the vapors from rising to your eyes.

3 tbsp	butter	45 mL
8 cups	thinly sliced Spanish onions (about 2 to 3)	2 L
1/4 tsp	dried thyme	1 mL
1/4 tsp	pepper	1 mL
2 tbsp	all-purpose flour	25 mL
6 cups	beef stock	1.5 L
1 tbsp	olive oil	15 mL
1	large garlic clove, minced	1
6	slices French bread, about 3/4-inch (2 cm) thick	6
2 cups	shredded Gruyere cheese	500 mL

1. In a Dutch oven or large heavy saucepan, melt butter over medium heat. Add onions, thyme and pepper; cook, stirring often, for 15 minutes or until onions are tender and a rich golden color. Blend in flour; stir in stock. Bring to a boil, stirring until thickened. Reduce heat to medium-low, cover and simmer for 15 minutes.

2. Meanwhile, position oven rack 6 inches (15 cm) from broiler; preheat broiler.

3. In a small bowl, combine olive oil and garlic; lightly brush oil mixture over both sides of bread. Arrange on baking sheet; place under broiler and toast on both sides.

4. Place toasts in deep ovenproof soup bowls; sprinkle with half the cheese. Arrange bowls in large shallow baking pan. Ladle hot soup in bowls. Sprinkle with remaining cheese. Place under broiler for 3 minutes or until cheese melts and is lightly browned. Serve immediately.

Old-Fashioned Pea Soup with Smoked Ham

Serves 8

My family came from the Netherlands to Southern Ontario in the 1950s and we were raised on this warming Dutch soup. When I moved to Quebec some 20 years ago, I discovered pea soup was also a key staple in that province's food heritage and I felt right at home.

TIP

For a wonderful rich flavor, I like to add a meaty ham bone to the soup as it simmers. As most hams sold today in supermarkets are boneless, however, the addition of both chopped smoked ham and chicken stock make a good substitute. Do add a ham bone, though, if you have one, and use water instead of stock. Smoked pork hock is another alternative if a ham bone is not available. Remove ham bone at end of cooking; scrape off any meat and add to soup.

2 tbsp	butter	25 mL
1	medium leek, white and light green part only, chopped	1
1	large onion, chopped	1
2	large cloves garlic, finely chopped	2
3	carrots, peeled and chopped	3
1	large stalk celery including leaves, chopped	1
1 1/2 tsp	dried marjoram	7 mL
1	bay leaf	1
1/4 tsp	pepper	1 mL
8 cups	chicken stock (approximate)	2 L
2 cups	chopped smoked ham	500 mL
1 1/2 cups	dried yellow or green split peas, rinsed and picked over	375 mL
	Salt	
1/4 cup	chopped fresh parsley	50 mL

1. In a Dutch oven or stockpot, melt butter over medium heat. Add leek, onion, garlic, carrots, celery, marjoram, bay leaf and pepper; cook, stirring often, for 8 minutes or until softened.

2. Stir in stock, ham and split peas. Bring to a boil; reduce heat, cover and simmer, stirring occasionally, for about 1 1/2 hours or until split peas are tender.

3. Remove bay leaf; Adjust seasoning with salt and pepper to taste. Stir in parsley. Soup thickens as it cools; thin with additional stock or water to desired consistency.

Creamy Tomato Soup

Serves 6

I always look forward to late summer — when baskets of lush ripe tomatoes are the showpiece in outdoor markets — so I can make this silky smooth soup. In winter, vine-ripened greenhouse tomatoes make a good stand-in, particularly if you use a little tomato paste for extra depth. Just add 1 to 2 tbsp (15 to 25 mL) when puréeing soup.

TIP

A sunny window sill may seem like the ideal place to ripen tomatoes, but hot blistering sun can end up baking them instead.
To ripen, place tomatoes in a paper bag and leave on the counter at room temperature. Never store tomatoes in the fridge; it numbs their delicate flavor.

Preheat oven to 400° F (200° C)

1 tbsp	olive oil	15 mL
6	ripe tomatoes (2 lbs [1 kg]), cored and quartered	6
1	medium leek, white and light green part only, chopped	1
1	small onion, coarsely chopped	1
2	medium carrots, peeled and coarsely chopped	2
1	stalk celery including leaves, chopped	1
2	large cloves garlic, sliced	2
1/2 tsp	salt	2 mL
1/4 tsp	pepper	1 mL
Pinch	nutmeg	Pinch
3 cups	chicken stock *or* vegetable stock (approximate)	750 mL
1 cup	light (15%) cream	250 mL
2 tbsp	chopped fresh herbs such as parsley, basil or chives	25 mL

1. Drizzle oil over bottom of a large shallow roasting pan. Add tomatoes, leek, onion, carrot, celery and garlic; season with salt, pepper and nutmeg.

2. Roast, uncovered, in preheated oven, stirring often, for 1 1/4 hours or until vegetables are very tender, but not brown.

3. Add 2 cups (500 mL) of the stock to pan; purée mixture in batches, preferably in a blender or a food processor, until very smooth. Strain soup through a sieve into large saucepan.

4. Add cream and enough of the remaining stock to thin soup to desired consistency. Adjust seasoning with salt and pepper to taste. Heat until piping hot; do not let the soup boil or it may curdle. Ladle into warm bowls; sprinkle with fresh herbs.

Hearty Beef-Barley Soup

Serves 12

I can't think of a better combination than thick slices of warm bread from the oven and steaming bowls of soup when you come in from the cold. This tried-and-true soup has a hearty beefy-mushroom taste and lots of old-fashioned appeal.

TIP

If I'm going to the trouble of making homemade soup, I like to make a big pot so there are plenty of leftovers for my freezer. Ladle soup into containers and freeze for up to 3 months.

1 tbsp	vegetable oil	15 mL
1 1/2 lbs	meaty beef shanks (2 or 3), trimmed of fat	750 g
1 lb	mushrooms, chopped	500 g
2	large onions, chopped	2
4	cloves garlic, finely chopped	4
2	bay leaves	2
2 tsp	salt	10 mL
1 tsp	dried thyme	5 mL
1/4 tsp	pepper	1 mL
12 cups	water	3 L
3/4 cup	pearl or pot barley, rinsed	175 mL
4	carrots, peeled and chopped	4
2	large stalks celery including leaves, chopped	2

1. In a Dutch oven or stockpot, heat oil over medium-high heat. Add beef and cook until nicely browned on both sides. Transfer to a plate.

2. Reduce heat to medium. Add mushrooms, onions, garlic, bay leaves, salt, thyme and pepper; cook, stirring often, for 5 minutes or until softened. Return beef to pan. Pour in water and bring to a boil. Reduce heat to medium-low and simmer, covered, stirring occasionally, for 1 hour.

3. Add barley, carrots and celery. Cover and simmer, stirring occasionally, for 1 hour more or until beef is tender.

4. Remove beef with slotted spoon. Discard bones; finely chop the meat and return to soup. Discard bay leaves; adjust seasoning with salt and pepper to taste.

Mediterranean Seafood Soup

Serves 6 as a main course or 8 to 10 as a starter

Here's an inviting soup that's fragrant with garlic and brimming with fresh seafood in a rich wine and tomato broth. It delivers pleasure from the first to the last spoonful. When I invite friends over for a relaxed dinner, I like to accompany this soup with crusty bread, followed by a simple salad and a fresh fruit dessert.

TIP

For a less expensive version of this recipe, replace shrimp and scallops with an equal quantity of mild fish. If using frozen fish in block form, remove packaging, place on plate and microwave at Medium for 5 minutes or until partly thawed. Cut into cubes; let stand for 15 minutes until completely thawed.

◆

For a change, try adding steamed mussels: Place 1 lb (500 g) mussels in a saucepan with 1/4 cup (50 mL) white wine or water. Place over high heat; cover and steam for 3 to 5 minutes or until shells open. Strain liquid and use as part of the fish stock called for in recipe. Discard any mussels that do not open. Add mussels to soup just before serving (leave in the shells, if desired).

2 tbsp	olive oil	25 mL
1	Spanish onion (about 1 lb [500 g]), chopped	1
3	cloves garlic, finely chopped	3
1	sweet red pepper, diced	1
1	sweet green pepper, diced	1
1	large stalk celery including leaves, chopped	1
1	bay leaf	1
1 tsp	salt	5 mL
1 tsp	paprika	5 mL
1/4 tsp	red pepper flakes	1 mL
1/4 tsp	saffron threads, crushed	1 mL
1	can (19 oz [540 mL]) tomatoes, chopped	1
4 cups	fish stock *or* chicken stock (approximate)	1 L
1 cup	dry white wine or vermouth *or* stock	250 mL
1 lb	halibut or other mild white fish, cubed	500 g
8 oz	raw medium shrimp, peeled and deveined, tails left on	250 g
8 oz	scallops, halved if large	250 g
1/3 cup	finely chopped fresh parsley	75 mL

1. In a Dutch oven or large saucepan, heat oil over medium-high heat. Add onion, garlic, peppers, celery, bay leaf, salt, paprika, red pepper flakes and saffron; cook, stirring often, for 5 minutes or until vegetables are softened.

2. Add tomatoes with juice, stock and wine. Bring to a boil; reduce heat to medium-low and simmer, covered, for 30 minutes. (Recipe can be prepared to this point up to a day ahead, or frozen for up to 3 months; when reheating, bring back to a full boil.)

3. Stir in halibut, shrimp, scallops and parsley; cover and simmer for 3 to 5 minutes or until fish is opaque. Serve immediately in warm soup bowls.

Chunky Minestrone

Serves 10 to 12

This nourishing soup is chockfull of vegetables and excels at chasing away the winter chills. It's soothing both to the body and the soul.

TIP

Chicken stock is one of the most indispensable flavoring agents in the kitchen. Commercial stock cubes and powders are loaded with salt and just don't deliver the flavor of homemade stock. But who has time to make stock from scratch these days? If you can spare 5 minutes, I'll tell you how I make my
Quick Chicken Stock:

Place 3 lbs (1.5 kg) chicken bones (such as neck, back-bones and wing tips) in a large stockpot. Cover with 10 cups (2.5 L) cold water. Add 1 large chopped onion, 2 chopped carrots, 1 large chopped celery stalk including leaves, 1/2 tsp (2 mL) dried thyme, 1 bay leaf, 1 tsp (5 mL) salt and pepper. Simmer, covered, for 2 hours; strain. Makes about 8 cups (2 L). Refrigerate for 3 days or freeze for up to 3 months in containers.

VARIATION

Chicken or Turkey Minestrone
Add 2 cups (500 mL) diced cooked chicken or turkey along with chickpeas. Extras of this soup freeze well for up to 3 months.

2 tbsp	olive oil	25 mL
2	medium onions, chopped	2
4	cloves garlic, finely chopped	4
3	medium carrots, peeled and diced	3
2	stalks celery including leaves, chopped	2
1 1/2 tsp	dried basil	7 mL
1 tsp	dried oregano *or* marjoram	5 mL
1/2 tsp	pepper	2 mL
10 cups	chicken stock *or* vegetable stock	2.5 L
1	can (19 oz [540 mL]) tomatoes, chopped	1
2 cups	small cauliflower florets *or* shredded cabbage	500 mL
1 1/2 cups	green beans, cut into 1-inch (2.5 cm) lengths	375 mL
3/4 cup	small-shaped pasta such as tubetti or shells	175 mL
1	can (19 oz [540 mL]) chickpeas *or* small white beans, rinsed and drained	1
1/3 cup	chopped fresh parsley	75 mL
	Freshly grated Parmesan cheese	

1. In a Dutch oven or large stockpot, heat oil over medium heat. Add onions, garlic, carrots, celery, basil, oregano and pepper; cook, stirring, for 5 minutes or until softened.

2. Stir in stock, tomatoes with juice, cauliflower and beans. Bring to a boil; reduce heat to medium-low and simmer, covered, for 20 minutes or until vegetables are tender.

3. Stir in pasta; cover and simmer for 10 minutes, stirring occasionally, until pasta is just tender.

4. Add chickpeas and parsley; cook 5 minutes more or until heated through. Ladle soup into heated bowls and sprinkle with Parmesan.

Black Bean and Corn Soup

Serves 6

My idea of a no-fuss dinner is this easy soup served with warm bread. It's especially reassuring to know that when I come home late from work, I can reach in my cupboard and pull out some convenient canned products — and dinner is on the table in no time!

Supermarkets are full of beans these days. With this recipe, why not try chickpeas, Romano or white kidney beans? Soups that call for canned products, such as tomatoes and beans, contain hefty quantities of salt (as do commercial stock bases) so be cautious about adding extra. Instead, rely on your pepper mill for a seasoning boost.

1 tbsp	olive oil	15 mL
1	medium onion, chopped	1
2	cloves garlic, minced	2
1	sweet green pepper, diced	1
1	large stalk celery, diced	1
1 tsp	dried oregano	5 mL
1 tsp	ground cumin	5 mL
1/2 tsp	dried thyme	2 mL
Pinch	cayenne pepper	Pinch
4 cups	chicken stock *or* vegetable stock	1 L
1	can (19 oz [540 mL]) tomatoes, chopped	1
1	can (19 oz [540 mL]) black beans, drained and rinsed	1
1 cup	corn niblets (fresh, frozen or canned)	250 mL
1 cup	diced smoked sausage, such as kielbasa, *or* smoked ham (optional)	250 mL
1/4 cup	chopped fresh coriander *or* parsley	50 mL

1. In a large saucepan, heat oil over medium-high heat. Add onion, garlic, pepper, celery, oregano, cumin, thyme and cayenne pepper; cook, stirring, for 5 minutes or until softened.

2. Add stock and tomatoes with juice; bring to a boil. Reduce heat to medium-low and simmer, covered, for 20 minutes.

3. Stir in beans, corn and sausage, if using. Cook 5 minutes more or until vegetables are tender. Stir in coriander; ladle into warm bowls.

Leek, Potato and Cabbage Soup

Serves 6 to 8

With all the glamorous foods out there now, the lowly cabbage is often neglected. That's a shame. Cabbage is an excellent partner to soothing potatoes and smoky sausage in this robust soup — which shows just how rich an addition this underrated vegetable can be. Taste it and you'll see.

TIP

Store soup in covered container in refrigerator for up to 5 days.

◆

To clean leeks, trim dark green tops. Cut down center almost to root end and chop. Rinse in a sink full of cold water to remove sand; scoop up leeks and place in colander to drain or use a salad spinner.

2 tbsp	olive oil	25 mL
2	medium leeks, white and light green part only, chopped	2
2	cloves garlic, finely chopped	2
1/4 tsp	pepper	1 mL
1/4 tsp	caraway seeds (optional)	1 mL
3	potatoes, such as Yukon Gold, peeled and cut into 1/2-inch (1 cm) cubes	3
4 cups	finely shredded green cabbage	1 L
6 cups	beef stock	1.5 L
8 oz	kielbasa, or other cooked smoked sausage, cut into 1/2-inch (1 cm) cubes	250 g
1/4 cup	chopped fresh parsley	50 mL

1. In a large saucepan, heat oil over medium heat. Add leeks, garlic, pepper and, if using, caraway seeds; cook, stirring, for 4 minutes or until softened.

2. Stir in potatoes, cabbage and stock. Bring to a boil; reduce heat to medium-low and simmer, covered, for 20 minutes or until vegetables are tender.

3. Add sausage and parsley; cook 5 minutes more or until sausage is heated through.

Curried Cream of Root Vegetable Soup

Serves 6

Here's a seductive soup with a Caribbean accent to serve for a special dinner. The surprising combination of earthy root vegetables, married with spices like ginger and curry, gives the soup a delicious Island flare. My friends always go home with the recipe.

TIP

The carrots, sweet potato and rutabaga, cut into 1/2-inch (1 cm) cubes, should total 4 cups (1 L).

◆

To add a decorative touch, ladle soup into warm bowls and drizzle top with cream or add small spoonfuls of sour cream or yogurt. Then use a skewer to draw a design on the surface for an interesting effect.

VARIATION

Curried Butternut Squash and Apple Soup
Substitute 5 cups (1.25 L) peeled and cubed butternut squash for the carrots, sweet potato and rutabaga.

2 tbsp	butter	25 mL
1 1/2 cups	peeled, diced apples	375 mL
1	medium onion, chopped	1
2	cloves garlic, minced	2
1 tbsp	minced ginger root	15 mL
1 1/2 tsp	curry powder	7 mL
1/2 tsp	ground cumin	2 mL
1/2 tsp	ground coriander	2 mL
1/4 tsp	dried thyme	1 mL
Pinch	cayenne pepper	Pinch
2	carrots, peeled and cubed	2
1	sweet potato, peeled and cubed	1
1 cup	cubed rutabaga	1
4 cups	chicken stock *or* vegetable stock	1 L
1 cup	light (15%) cream	250 mL
1/4 cup	chopped fresh coriander *or* parsley	50 mL

1. In a large saucepan, heat butter over medium heat. Add apples, onion, garlic, ginger root, curry powder, cumin, coriander, thyme and cayenne pepper; cook, stirring, for 5 minutes or until softened.

2. Add carrots, sweet potato, rutabaga and stock. Bring to a boil; reduce heat to medium-low and simmer, covered, for 30 minutes or until vegetables are very tender. Let cool slightly.

3. In a blender or a food processor, purée soup in batches until smooth. Return to saucepan; stir in cream and heat through. Do not allow soup to boil or it may curdle. Ladle into bowls; sprinkle with coriander.

Chicken Noodle Soup

Serves 8

Often called "Jewish penicillin," chicken soup is the perfect antidote to an oncoming cold. But there's more to its restorative powers. Rich and delicious, it can banish the winter blues and make you feel just plain good any day of the year.

TIP

You don't have to slave over the stove to make this soul-satisfying soup. Adding the chicken and the vegetables to the pot at the same time streamlines the process and does away with the chore of making stock first. The results are every bit as pleasing.

3 lb	whole chicken or chicken pieces, such as legs and breasts	1.5 kg
10 cups	water (approximate)	2.5 L
1	large onion, finely chopped	1
3	carrots, peeled and chopped	3
2	stalks celery including leaves, chopped	2
2 tbsp	chopped fresh parsley	25 mL
1/2 tsp	dried thyme	2 mL
2 tsp	salt	10 mL
1/4 tsp	pepper	1 mL
1	bay leaf	1
2 cups	medium or broad egg noodles	500 mL
1 cup	finely diced zucchini *or* small cauliflower florets	250 mL
2 tbsp	chopped fresh dill *or* parsley	25 mL

1. Rinse chicken; remove as much skin and excess fat as possible. Place in a large stockpot; add water to cover. Bring to a boil over high heat; using a slotted spoon, skim off foam as it rises to the surface.

2. Add onion, carrots, celery, parsley, thyme, salt, pepper and bay leaf. Reduce heat to medium-low; cover and simmer for about 1 1/4 hours or until chicken is tender.

3. Remove chicken with slotted spoon and place in a large bowl; let cool slightly. Pull chicken meat off the bones, discarding skin and bones. Cut meat into bite-sized pieces. Reserve 2 cups (500 mL) for soup. (Use remainder for casseroles and sandwiches.)

4. Skim fat from surface of soup; bring to a boil. Add cubed chicken, noodles, zucchini and dill; cook for 10 minutes or until noodles and vegetables are tender. Remove bay leaf. Adjust seasoning with salt and pepper to taste.

Cheddar Broccoli Chowder

Serves 6

My vegetarian daughter loves this soup and so do I. It's no-fuss to prepare, easy to reheat and makes a complete meal. With a vegetarian in the family, this is a recipe I count on.

TIP

Depending on what I have in the fridge, I make variations on this versatile, tasty soup by using other vegetables, such as carrots and cauliflower.

2 tbsp	butter	25 mL
1	small onion, finely chopped	1
1/4 cup	all-purpose flour	50 mL
3 cups	vegetable stock *or* chicken stock	750 mL
2 cups	potatoes, peeled and cut into 1/2-inch (1 cm) cubes	500 mL
1	bay leaf	1
3 cups	finely chopped broccoli florets and peeled stalks	750 mL
1 1/2 cups	milk	375 mL
1 1/2 cups	shredded Cheddar cheese	375 mL
	Pepper	

1. Melt butter in a large saucepan over medium heat. Cook onion, stirring, for 2 minutes or until softened. Blend in flour; stir in stock. Bring to a boil, stirring, until thickened.

2. Add potatoes and bay leaf; reduce heat, cover and simmer, stirring occasionally, for 10 minutes.

3. Add broccoli; simmer, stirring occasionally, for 10 minutes more or until vegetables are tender.

4. Stir in milk and cheese; heat just until cheese melts and soup is piping hot. Do not let the soup boil or it may curdle. Remove bay leaf; adjust seasoning with pepper to taste.

Clam Chowder

Serves 4

Thick and creamy, laden with chunks of potatoes and featuring the smoky flavor of bacon, this restaurant favorite is easy to recreate in your home kitchen.

VARIATION

Fish Chowder

Omit canned clams. Increase fish stock to 2 cups (500 mL). Add 12 oz (375 g) cubed fish such as cod, haddock or bluefish at end of cooking along with bacon bits. Simmer for 5 minutes or until fish flakes. Add more stock, if necessary, to thin soup to desired consistency.

4	slices bacon, chopped	4
1	can (5 oz [142 g]) clams, drained, juice reserved	1
1	small onion, finely chopped	1
1	stalk celery, finely diced	1
1	clove garlic, minced	1
1	bay leaf	1
1 1/2 cups	potatoes, peeled, cut into 1/2-inch (1 cm) cubes	375 mL
1 cup	fish stock *or* chicken stock	250 mL
2 cups	milk	500 mL
3 tbsp	all-purpose flour	45 mL
2 tbsp	finely chopped fresh parsley	25 mL
	Salt and pepper	

1. In a large saucepan, cook bacon over medium heat, stirring, for 4 minutes or until crisp. Remove; blot with paper towels and set aside.

2. Add drained clams, onion, celery, garlic and bay leaf; cook, stirring often, for 3 minutes or until vegetables are softened.

3. Stir in reserved clam juice, potatoes and stock; bring to a boil. Reduce heat to medium-low, cover and simmer for 15 minutes or until vegetables are tender.

4. In a bowl, blend a small amount of the milk into the flour to make a smooth paste. Stir in remaining milk until smooth and lump-free. Add to saucepan; bring to a boil over medium-high heat, stirring often, until mixture thickens.

5. Stir in bacon bits and parsley; season with salt, if needed, and pepper to taste. Remove bay leaf before serving.

MAIN DISHES

Old-Fashioned Beef Stew

Serves 4 to 6

What's more comforting than a satisfying stew? You start feeling good the minute you set this one-pot dish to simmer on the stovetop. As the herb-infused aroma wafts through your kitchen the good feeling grows. The first forkful confirms that this stew is comfort food at its best. What's more, it can comfort you all over again the next day with easy-to-reheat leftovers. Delicious served with crusty bread to mop up the flavorful sauce.

TIP

To give your stew a rich, dark color, leave meat out of the refrigerator for 20 minutes; blot with paper towels before browning. Cook beef in small batches for best browning and reheat pan before adding each new batch of meat. I find fresh meat browns better than frozen meat that has been defrosted.

◆

A word about parsley. Use either the curly leaf variety or the more strongly flavored flat-leaf type. Wash well in plenty of water to remove dirt; dry parsley in a salad spinner or wrap in clean towel. The drier the parsley, the longer it lasts in your refrigerator. Wrap in paper towels, then in a plastic bag and refrigerate. To save time, every few weeks I finely

Continued next page

1/4 cup	all-purpose flour	50 mL
1 tsp	salt	5 mL
1/2 tsp	pepper	2 mL
2 tbsp	vegetable oil (approximate)	25 mL
1 1/2 lbs	stewing beef, cut into cubes 1 1/2 inches (4 cm) square	750 g
2	medium onions, chopped	2
3	cloves garlic, finely chopped	3
1 tsp	dried thyme	5 mL
1 tsp	dried marjoram	5 mL
1	bay leaf	1
1 cup	red wine *or* additional beef stock	250 mL
3 tbsp	tomato paste	45 mL
3 cups	beef stock (approximate)	750 mL
5	carrots	5
2	stalks celery	2
1 1/2 lbs	potatoes (about 5)	750 g
12 oz	green beans	375 g
1/4 cup	chopped fresh parsley	50 mL

1. Combine flour, salt and pepper in a heavy plastic bag. In batches, add beef to flour mixture and toss to coat. Transfer to a plate. Reserve remaining flour mixture.

2. In a Dutch oven, heat half the oil over medium-high heat; cook beef in batches, adding more oil as needed, until browned all over. Transfer to a plate.

3. Reduce heat to medium-low. Add onions, garlic, thyme, marjoram, bay leaf and remaining flour to pan; cook, stirring, for 4 minutes or until softened. Add wine and tomato paste; cook, stirring, to scrape up brown bits. Return beef and any accumulated juices to pan; pour in stock.

4. Bring to a boil, stirring, until slightly thickened. Reduce heat, cover and simmer over medium-low heat, stirring occasionally, for 1 hour.

Continued from previous page

chop a few bunches of parsley, pack into a container and freeze. Though not suitable for fresh salads, the frozen parsley is perfect to add to soups, stews, meatloaves and casseroles.

5. Meanwhile, peel carrots and halve lengthwise. Cut carrots and celery into 1 1/2-inch (4 cm) chunks. Peel potatoes and quarter. Add vegetables to pan. Cover and simmer for 30 minutes.

6. Trim ends of beans and cut into 2-inch (5 cm) lengths. Stir into stew mixture, adding more stock if necessary, until vegetables are just covered. Cover and simmer for 30 minutes more or until vegetables are tender. Remove bay leaf and stir in parsley. Adjust seasoning with salt and pepper to taste.

Pot Roast with Beer and Caramelized Onions

Serves 8

When I was growing up, pot roasts were a staple in my house. I can remember coming home from school to the tantalizing smell of a roast slowly braising in the oven. This recipe features a richly colored sauce from caramelized onions and a subtle sweet-sour taste from the beer and brown sugar. It's delicious served with creamy mashed potatoes or egg noodles.

Preheat oven to 325° F (160° C)

3 to 4 lbs	beef pot roast such as cross-rib, rump or brisket	1.5 to 2 kg
1/4 cup	all-purpose flour	50 mL
2 tbsp	vegetable oil (approximate)	25 mL
4	medium onions, halved lengthwise and thinly sliced (about 1 1/4 lbs [625 g])	4
2 tbsp	brown sugar	25 mL
2	bay leaves	2
1 tsp	salt	5 mL
1/2 tsp	ground cinnamon	2 mL
1/2 tsp	ground ginger	2 mL
1/2 tsp	pepper	2 mL
3	large cloves garlic, finely chopped	3
2 tbsp	balsamic vinegar	25 mL
1	bottle (12 oz [341 mL]) beer	1
1	can (7 1/2 oz [213 mL]) tomato sauce	1
1 1/2 lbs	carrots (about 8)	750 g
1	small rutabaga (about 1 lb [500 g])	1

1. On a large plate, roll meat in flour to coat. Shake off excess; reserve.

2. In a Dutch oven, heat half the oil over medium-high heat. Brown meat on all sides, about 6 minutes. Transfer to a plate.

3. Reduce heat to medium. Add remaining oil to Dutch oven. Add onions, brown sugar, bay leaves, salt, cinnamon, ginger and pepper; cook, stirring often, for 12 to 15 minutes or until onions are softened and nicely colored. (Add more oil, if needed, to prevent onions from burning.)

4. Add reserved flour and garlic; cook, stirring, for 30 seconds. Add vinegar; cook until evaporated. Pour in beer and tomato sauce; bring to a boil, stirring, until thickened. Return meat and accumulated juices to pan. Cover and roast in preheated oven for 2 hours.

5. Meanwhile, peel carrots and rutabaga; cut into 2- by 1/2-inch (5 by 1 cm) strips. Add to beef. Cover and cook 1 to 1 1/2 hours more or until meat is tender.

6. Remove roast from pan; cut into thin slices. Arrange on serving platter; surround with vegetables. Skim any fat from sauce; spoon some sauce over meat and pour the rest into a warmed sauceboat to serve on the side.

Best-Ever Meat Loaf

Serves 6

I could make this juicy meat loaf with garlic mashed potatoes every week and never hear a complaint from my family that it's served too often.

TIP

I like to use oatmeal as a binder, since it gives a coarser texture to the meat loaf (bread crumbs produce a finer one). Use whichever binder you prefer.

◆

I always double the recipe and wrap the extra cooked meat loaf in plastic wrap, then in foil, for the freezer. Defrost overnight in the fridge. To reheat, cut into slices and place in saucepan. Moisten with about 1/2 cup (125 mL) beef stock; set over medium heat until piping hot. Or place meat loaf and stock in casserole dish and microwave at Medium until heated through.

Preheat oven to 350° F (180° C)
9- by 5-inch (2 L) loaf pan

1 tbsp	vegetable oil	15 mL
1	medium onion, chopped	1
2	cloves garlic, minced	2
1 tsp	dried basil	5 mL
1 tsp	dried marjoram	5 mL
3/4 tsp	salt	4 mL
1/4 tsp	pepper	1 mL
1	egg	1
1/4 cup	chili sauce *or* ketchup	50 mL
1 tbsp	Worcestershire sauce	15 mL
2 tbsp	chopped fresh parsley	25 mL
1 1/2 lbs	lean ground beef	750 g
3/4 cup	rolled oats	175 mL
	or	
1/2 cup	dry bread crumbs	125 mL

1. In a large nonstick skillet, heat oil over medium heat. Add onion, garlic, basil, marjoram, salt and pepper; cook, stirring, for 3 minutes or until softened. (Or place in microwave-safe bowl; microwave, covered, at High for 3 minutes.) Let cool slightly.

2. In a large bowl, beat the egg; stir in onion mixture, chili sauce, Worcestershire sauce and parsley. Crumble beef over mixture and sprinkle with rolled oats. Using a wooden spoon or with your hands, gently mix until evenly combined.

3. Pack meat mixture lightly into loaf pan. Bake in pre-heated oven for 1 hour or until meat thermometer registers 170° F (75° C). Let stand for 5 minutes; drain fat in pan, turn out onto a plate and cut into thick slices.

Amazing Chili

Serves 6 to 8

Every cook has a special version of chili. Here's mine — it's meaty and nicely spiced with just the right amount of beans. Not everyone agrees that beans belong in a chili — witness the Texas version dubbed "bowl of red" — but I love the way the beans absorb the spices and rich tomato flavor.

TIP

The flavor of the chili hinges on the quality of chili powder used. Most powders are a blend of dried, ground mild chilies, as well as cumin, oregano, garlic and salt. Read the list of ingredients to be sure you're not buying one with starch and sugar fillers. Chili powder should not be confused with powdered or ground chilies of the cayenne pepper variety.

1 1/2 lbs	lean ground beef	750 g
2	medium onions, chopped	2
3	cloves garlic, finely chopped	3
2	stalks celery, chopped	2
1	large sweet green pepper, chopped	1
2 tbsp	chili powder	25 mL
1 1/2 tsp	dried oregano	7 mL
1 1/2 tsp	ground cumin	7 mL
1 tsp	salt	5 mL
1/2 tsp	red pepper flakes, or to taste	2 mL
1	can (28 oz [796 mL]) tomatoes, chopped, juice reserved	1
1 cup	beef stock	250 mL
1	can (19 oz [540 mL]) pinto *or* red kidney beans, drained and rinsed	1
1/4 cup	chopped fresh parsley *or* coriander	50 mL

1. In a Dutch oven, brown beef over medium-high heat, breaking up with back of a spoon, for about 7 minutes or until no longer pink.

2. Reduce heat to medium. Add onions, garlic, celery, green pepper, chili powder, oregano, cumin, salt and red pepper flakes; cook, stirring often, for 5 minutes or until vegetables are softened.

3. Stir in the tomatoes with juice and the stock. Bring to a boil; reduce heat, cover and simmer, stirring occasionally, for 1 hour.

4. Add beans and parsley; cover and simmer for 10 minutes more.

Shepherd's Pie

Serves 6

Mushrooms add a depth of flavor to this dish and help cut down on the amount of meat used. When my children were young and didn't like the sight of mushrooms in their favorite supper dish, I would finely chop the mushrooms in a food processor and they never knew the difference.

TIP

Unless you're using expensive tomato paste from a tube, what do you do with leftover canned tomato paste? You can freeze leftover tomato paste in ice-cube trays, but I prefer to drop tablespoonfuls (you'll get 10 from a 5 1/2 oz [156 mL] can) onto a baking sheet lined with plastic wrap and freeze. When firm, transfer to a plastic storage bag or container and place in freezer. What's nice about this method is that you need only add the already-measured amount to your recipe.

Preheat oven to 375° F (190° C)
Shallow 12- by 8-inch (2.5 L) baking dish

1 lb	lean ground beef *or* ground veal	500 g
8 oz	mushrooms, sliced or chopped	250 g
1	medium onion, finely chopped	1
2	cloves garlic, minced	2
1/2 tsp	dried thyme	2 mL
1/2 tsp	dried marjoram	2 mL
3 tbsp	all-purpose flour	50 mL
1 1/2 cups	beef stock	375 mL
2 tbsp	tomato paste	25 mL
2 tsp	Worcestershire sauce	10 mL
	Salt and pepper	
1	can (12 oz [341 mL]) corn niblets, drained	1
2 lbs	potatoes (about 6 medium), peeled and cubed	1 kg
3/4 cup	milk *or* buttermilk	175 mL
2 tbsp	dry bread crumbs	25 mL
2 tbsp	Parmesan cheese	25 mL
1/4 tsp	paprika	1 mL

1. In a large nonstick skillet, cook beef over medium-high heat, breaking up with back of a spoon, for 5 minutes or until no longer pink.

2. Add mushrooms, onion, garlic, thyme and marjoram; cook, stirring often, for 5 minutes or until softened. Sprinkle with flour; stir in stock, tomato paste and Worcestershire sauce. Bring to a boil; reduce heat and simmer, covered, for 8 minutes. Season with salt, if necessary, and pepper to taste.

3. Spread meat mixture in baking dish; layer with corn.

4. Meanwhile, in a large saucepan of boiling salted water, cook potatoes until tender. Drain and mash using a potato masher or electric mixer; beat in milk until smooth. Season with salt and pepper to taste. Place small spoonfuls of potato over corn and spread evenly. (The recipe can be prepared up to this point earlier in the day or the day before, then covered and refrigerated.)

5. In a small bowl, combine bread crumbs, Parmesan and paprika; sprinkle over top of shepherd's pie.

6. Bake in preheated oven for 25 to 30 minutes (40 minutes, if refrigerated) or until filling is bubbly.

Thyme-Roasted Chicken with Garlic Gravy

Serves 4

I feel like it's a special occasion when I have a roast chicken in the oven. It conjures up a homey smell and feel. In my opinion, it's one of the most satisfying dishes on earth.

Here we place herbs and seasonings under the bird's skin to produce a succulent, flavorful chicken. Slow roasting with lots of garlic creates a wonderful aroma — yet, surprisingly, imparts only a subtle flavor to the gravy.

TIP

In a rush to roast a chicken? Increase oven temperature to 400° F (200° C) and roast bird for about 1 1/4 hours. Make sure to add extra stock to the pan — it evaporates during roasting — and baste bird often.

Preheat oven to 325° F (160° C)
Roasting pan with rack

1	chicken (about 3 1/2 lbs [1.75 kg])	1
10	cloves garlic, peeled	10
1 tsp	dried thyme	5 mL
1/4 tsp	salt	1 mL
1/4 tsp	pepper	1 mL
1 1/4 cups	chicken stock	300 mL
1/2 cup	white wine *or* additional chicken stock	125 mL
1 tbsp	all-purpose flour	15 mL

1. Remove giblets and neck from chicken. Rinse and pat dry chicken inside and out. Place 2 cloves garlic inside cavity. Starting at cavity opening, gently lift skin and rub thyme, salt and pepper over breasts and legs. Tie legs together with string; tuck wings under back.

2. Add remaining garlic, half the chicken stock and the wine to roasting pan; place chicken, breast side up, on rack in pan.

3. Roast in preheated oven, basting every 30 minutes, adding additional stock if pan juices evaporate, for 1 3/4 to 2 hours or until pan juices run clear when chicken is pierced and meat thermometer inserted in thigh registers 185° F (85° C).

4. Transfer to a platter; tent with foil and let stand for 10 minutes before carving. Meanwhile, strain pan juices into measure, pressing down firmly to mash garlic into juices; skim off fat. Add enough of remaining stock to make 3/4 cup (175 mL).

5. In a small saucepan, stir together 2 tbsp (25 mL) of pan juices and flour; cook, stirring, over medium heat for 1 minute. Gradually whisk in remaining pan juices; cook, stirring, until boiling and thickened. Serve with chicken.

Rosemary Chicken Breasts with Layered Potatoes and Onions

Serves 4

A breeze to prepare, this easy-to-assemble dish is elegant enough to serve to company. The herb and lemon butter tucked under the skins keeps the chicken moist and I love the way it imparts a wonderful flavor to the vegetables layered on the bottom.

TIP

Make extra batches of rosemary butter, shape into small logs, wrap in plastic and store in the freezer. Cut into slices and use to tuck under the breast skins of whole roasting chickens or Cornish hens, or to top grilled meats.

Preheat oven to 375° F (190° C)
13- by 9-inch (3 L) shallow baking dish, oiled

3	medium potatoes (about 1 lb [500 g])	3
2	small sweet potatoes (about 1 lb [500 g])	2
1	medium onion	1
1 tsp	dried rosemary, crumbled	5 mL
	Salt and pepper to taste	
4	single chicken breasts with skin	4

Rosemary butter:

2 tbsp	butter	25 mL
1	large clove garlic, minced	1
1 tsp	grated lemon rind	5 mL
1 tsp	dried rosemary, crumbled	5 mL
1/4 tsp	salt	1 mL
1/4 tsp	pepper	1 mL

1. Peel potatoes, sweet potatoes and onion; cut into very thin slices. Layer vegetables in prepared baking dish. Season with rosemary, salt and pepper.

2. Place whole chicken breasts, skin side up, on work surface. (If you purchased whole breasts with backs on, cut away back bone using poultry shears.) Remove any fat deposits under skins. Press down on breast bone to flatten slightly.

3. Make the rosemary butter: In a small bowl, mash together butter, garlic, lemon rind, rosemary, salt and pepper. Divide into 4 portions.

4. Carefully loosen the breast skins and tuck rosemary butter under skins, patting to distribute evenly.

5. Arrange chicken on top of vegetables in baking dish. Cover with sheet of greased foil; roast in preheated oven for 45 minutes. Uncover and roast 25 to 30 minutes more or until vegetables are tender and chicken is nicely colored.

Chicken-Vegetable Cobbler

Serves 6

Some dishes never lose their appeal — like this old-fashioned favorite, which is perfect to make on a lazy Sunday afternoon. It requires a little time to prepare, but once the creamy chicken mixture and its golden biscuit crust is bubbling away in the oven, you'll be glad you made the effort. And so will your family.

TIP

I've chosen a biscuit crust to make this a cobbler, but you can cover the savory chicken filling with your favorite pie pastry or frozen puff pastry to make a pot pie. Or you can omit the topping altogether and serve over rice or noodles.

◆

The chicken-vegetable mixture without the crust freezes well for up to 3 months.

◆

Fine herbs, available in the spice section of your grocery store, contains dried parsley, chives, tarragon and chervil. You can also use an Italian herb mix of basil, oregano and marjoram.

Preheat oven to 400° F (200° C)
12-cup (3 L) deep casserole dish

2 lbs	chicken legs, with thighs, skin and excess fat removed	1 kg
3 1/2 cups	water	850 mL
1 tsp	salt	5 mL
	Pepper to taste	
1	bay leaf	1
2 tbsp	butter	25 mL
2 cups	quartered mushrooms	500 mL
1	medium onion, chopped	1
1	large garlic clove, minced	1
2 tsp	dried fine herbs *or* dried basil	10 mL
1/3 cup	all-purpose flour	75 mL
3	carrots, peeled and sliced	3
2	stalks celery, chopped	2
1/2 cup	whipping (35%) cream *or* light (15%) cream	125 mL
1 cup	frozen peas	250 mL
1/4 cup	chopped fresh parsley	50 mL
	Salt and pepper to taste	
	CHEDDAR BISCUIT CRUST (recipe follows)	

1. In a large saucepan, combine chicken, water, salt, pepper and bay leaf. Bring to a boil; reduce heat to medium-low, cover and simmer for 1 hour. Let stand until chicken is cool enough to handle. Pull chicken meat from bones; cut into bite-sized pieces. Strain stock, skim off any fat; there should be 2 1/2 cups (625 mL) of stock. Add water, if necessary. Discard bay leaf.

2. In large saucepan, melt butter over medium heat; cook mushrooms, onions, garlic and fine herbs, stirring often, for 5 minutes or until softened.

3. Blend flour with small amount of stock until smooth; add rest of stock. Stir into mushroom mixture; bring to a boil, stirring, until thickened and smooth.

4. Add carrots and celery; cover and simmer over low heat, stirring occasionally, for 15 minutes or until vegetables are just tender.

5. Add chicken, cream, peas and parsley; season with salt and pepper to taste. Heat through. Spoon hot chicken mixture into casserole dish.

6. Meanwhile make biscuit crust (see below). Roll out on lightly floured board to make a circle large enough to cover casserole. Arrange on top of hot chicken mixture. (If making chicken mixture ahead, cover and refrigerate; microwave at Medium-High, or reheat in saucepan on stovetop until piping hot before topping with crust.)

7. Bake in preheated oven for about 25 to 30 minutes or until crust is golden and filling is bubbly.

CHEDDAR BISCUIT CRUST

1 1/3 cups	all-purpose flour	325 mL
2 tsp	baking powder	10 mL
1/2 tsp	baking soda	2 mL
1/4 tsp	salt	1 mL
1/2 cup	shredded Cheddar cheese (optional)	125 mL
1/2 cup	buttermilk	125 mL
1/4 cup	butter, melted	50 mL

1. In a bowl combine flour, baking powder, baking soda and salt. Add cheese, if using. Combine buttermilk and butter; stir into flour mixture to make a soft dough.

Roast Turkey with Sage-Bread Stuffing

Serves 8 to 10, plus leftovers

Turkey always has the place of honor when my family and friends gather for holiday meals. It's perfect when serving a crowd. It's economical, too, and everyone loves it. Best of all are the leftovers that get wrapped and placed in the fridge for hearty sandwiches the next day — or even later that night.

TIP

I prefer to roast a fresh turkey rather than a frozen bird (which is less moist and juicy.) To streamline the preparations, I've done away with stuffing the turkey. Instead, the stuffing is packed into a casserole dish and baked in the oven for the last hour of roasting the bird.

◆

Not sure what size turkey to buy? Estimate 1 lb (500 g) per person.

◆

Leave turkey (fresh or frozen) in original wrapping; place on tray and refrigerate promptly. (Tray prevents dripping juices from contaminating other foods.)

◆

Do not defrost turkey at room temperature; defrost in refrigerator and allow 5 hours per lb (10 hours per kg). This can take several days, depending on size of the bird.

Turkey tips continue, page 64...

Preheat oven to 325° F (160° C)
12-cup (3 L) casserole dish, greased
Shallow roasting pan or broiler pan, with greased rack

Stuffing:

1/3 cup	butter	75 mL
2 cups	chopped onions	500 mL
2 cups	chopped celery	500 mL
8 oz	mushrooms, chopped	250 g
4	cloves garlic, minced	4
1 tbsp	dried rubbed sage	15 mL
1 tsp	dried thyme	5 mL
1 tsp	dried marjoram	5 mL
1 tsp	salt	5 mL
1/2 tsp	pepper	2 mL
12 cups	white or whole bread cubes toasted on baking sheet in 350° F (180° C) oven for 15 minutes	3 L
1/2 cup	chopped fresh parsley	125 mL
1 cup	turkey stock (approximate)	250 mL

Turkey:

1	turkey, about 12 to 14 lbs (6 to 7 kg)	1
2 tbsp	melted butter	25 mL
6	cloves garlic, unpeeled	6
1	large onion, cut into 8 wedges	1
2	carrots, cut into chunks	2
1	large stalk celery, cut into chunks	1
1 tsp	dried rosemary, crumbled	5 mL
1/2 tsp	dried thyme	2 mL
1/2 tsp	dried marjoram	2 mL
	Salt and pepper	
1/2 cup	white wine	125 mL
1/4 cup	all-purpose flour	50 mL
3 cups	turkey stock	750 mL

Turkey Gravy Stock

Pat neck and giblets dry. (Do not use liver). In large saucepan, heat 1 tbsp (15 mL) vegetable oil over medium-high heat; cook neck and giblets, stirring, for 8 minutes or until nicely browned. Add 1 each chopped onion, carrot and celery stalk including leaves along with 1 tsp (5 mL) dried thyme; cook, stirring for 3 minutes or until vegetables are lightly colored. Add 1 cup (250 mL) white wine, if desired. Stir in 6 cups (1.5 L) water; season lightly with salt and pepper. Bring to boil, cover and simmer over medium-low heat for 3 hours. Strain stock through cheese-cloth-lined or fine sieve; discard solids.

Makes about 4 cups (1 L) stock

VARIATION

Sausage-Apple Stuffing

Cook 1 lb (500 g) bulk sausage meat in a large skillet over medium-high heat, breaking up with back of spoon, until no longer pink; drain off fat. Add 2 peeled, finely chopped apples; combine with bread stuffing mixture.

1. Make the stuffing: In a large nonstick skillet, melt butter over medium heat; add onions, celery, mushrooms, garlic, sage, thyme, marjoram, salt and pepper; cook, stirring often, for 15 minutes or until vegetables are tender.

2. In a large bowl, combine onion mixture, bread cubes and parsley. Spoon into prepared casserole dish. (Recipe can be prepared to this point up to 1 day ahead and refrigerated.)

3. To bake, add enough turkey stock to moisten stuffing and toss. (If you plan to stuff the bird, omit stock.) Cover with lid or foil and place in oven for the last hour of roasting turkey, uncovering for last 30 minutes to brown and crisp the top.

4. Prepare the turkey: Remove neck and giblets from bird; reserve to make stock. Rinse turkey with cold water; pat dry. Secure legs by tying with string or tuck under skin around the tail; fold wings back and secure neck skin with skewer.

5. Place turkey, breast side up, on rack in roasting pan. Brush bird with melted butter. Lightly crush garlic with side of knife; scatter garlic, onion, carrots and celery in pan. (This is optional but makes for a tasty gravy.) Season turkey and vegetables with rosemary, thyme, marjoram, salt and pepper.

6. Insert meat thermometer into thickest part of inner turkey thigh being careful not to touch bone. Roast turkey for 3 1/4 to 3 1/2 hours; no need to baste. (If turkey starts to brown too quickly, tent bird loosely with heavy-duty foil, shiny side down.) Turkey is done when meat thermometer registers 170° F (77° C) for unstuffed bird; 180° F (82° C) if stuffed. (The drumstick and breast feel soft and legs move easily when twisted.)

7. Remove from oven; cover with foil and let stand for 15 minutes for easy carving.

8. Skim fat from roasting pan; place over medium heat. Stir in flour; cook, stirring, for 1 minute. Add wine, if using; cook, stirring, until reduced by half. Stir in stock; bring to boil, scraping up brown bits from bottom of pan, until gravy thickens. Strain through a fine sieve into a saucepan, pressing down on vegetables; discard the vegetables. Season gravy with salt and pepper to taste.

TURKEY TIPS

Quick defrosting method

Place frozen turkey (in original wrapping) in cold water and change water frequently. Allow 1 hour per lb (2 hours per kg). Once defrosted, cook turkey within 2 days.

◆

Wash hands well before and after handling turkey. Wash and disinfect work surface and utensils with hot soapy water and dry thoroughly.

◆

Cook turkey thoroughly. Never slow roast at low temperatures or partially cook a bird, then continue roasting later on in day or next day.

◆

Roast in a 325° F (160° C) oven until a meat thermometer, inserted in the thickest portion of inner thigh, reaches an internal temperature of 170° F (77° C) for unstuffed bird; 180° F (82° C) for stuffed bird.

◆

Chill leftovers promptly. Do not leave cooked turkey at room temperature for more than 2 hours. Place cooked turkey meat in a casserole or wrap in foil or plastic and refrigerate immediately. Leftovers will keep in fridge for up to 4 days or freeze for 1 month.

WHOLE TURKEY ROASTING TIMES

Today's leaner turkeys take less time to cook than in the past. Don't rely on outdated information from old cookbooks and recipes. Here are newly revised roasting times:

Weight	Cooking time (hours) in 325° F (160° C) oven	
	Stuffed	Unstuffed
6 to 8 lbs (3 to 3.5 kg)	3 to 3 1/4	2 1/2 to 2 3/4
8 to 10 lbs (3.5 to 4.5 kg)	3 1/4 to 3 1/2	2 3/4 to 3
10 to 12 lbs (4.5 to 5.5 kg)	3 1/2 to 3 3/4	3 to 3 1/4
12 to 16 lbs (5.5 to 7 kg)	3 3/4 to 4	3 1/4 to 3 1/2
16 to 22 lbs) (7 to 10 kg	4 to 4 1/2	3 1/2 to 4

CREAMY TOMATO SOUP (PAGE 38) ➤

OVERLEAF: ZESTY BARBECUED SPARERIBS (PAGE 69) ➤

Rosemary Roast Lamb with New Potatoes

Serves 8

Lamb is often my first choice when planning a special dinner. It's always a crowd pleaser. I love the heavenly aroma of garlic and rosemary in this recipe — it fills my house and makes an especially warm welcome for friends as they come through the door.

TIP

Take the lamb out of the fridge about 30 minutes before roasting.

◆

Choose potatoes that are the same size so they roast evenly.

◆

As for the white wine, if you don't want to open a bottle, a good substitute is dry white vermouth. Keep a bottle handy in the cupboard for those recipes that call for white wine.

Preheat oven to 350° F (180° C)
Large, shallow roasting pan, oiled

1	leg of lamb, 5 to 6 lbs (2.5 to 3 kg)	1
8	cloves garlic	8
	Grated rind and juice of 1 lemon	
2 tbsp	olive oil	25 mL
1 tbsp	dried rosemary, crumbled	15 mL
1/2 tsp	salt	2 mL
1/2 tsp	pepper	2 mL
3 lbs	whole new potatoes, scrubbed (about 12)	1.5 kg
1 tbsp	all-purpose flour	15 mL
1/2 cup	white wine	125 mL
1 cup	chicken stock	250 mL

1. Cut 6 cloves garlic into 8 to 10 slivers each. Using the tip of a knife, cut shallow slits all over lamb and insert a garlic sliver into each.

2. Finely chop remaining 2 garlic cloves. In a bowl, combine garlic, lemon juice and rind, oil, rosemary, salt and pepper. Place lamb in prepared roasting pan; surround with potatoes. Brush lamb and potatoes generously with lemon-garlic mixture; Insert meat thermometer into thickest part of leg.

3. Roast in preheated oven for about 1 1/2 hours, turning potatoes over halfway through roasting, until meat thermometer registers 135° F (57° C) for medium-rare. (For medium, remove the potatoes and continue to roast lamb for 15 to 20 minutes more or to your liking.)

4. Remove lamb to a platter; tent with foil and let rest 10 minutes before carving. Transfer potatoes to a dish; keep warm.

5. Skim fat in pan; place over medium heat. Stir in flour and cook, stirring, until lightly colored. Pour in wine; cook, scraping up any brown bits until wine is reduced by half. Stir in stock; bring to a boil, stirring, until thickened. Strain through a fine sieve into a warm sauceboat.

6. Carve the lamb. Arrange slices on serving plate and moisten with some of the sauce; surround with roasted potatoes. Serve with remaining sauce.

≺ CHICKEN-VEGETABLE COBBLER (PAGE 60)

Company Pork Roast with Fruit Stuffing

Serves 8

I love the way the sweetness of dried fruit accents the delicate taste of pork in this recipe. And when you stuff the loin with a fruit and spice mixture, you ensure that the meat will be extra moist and flavorful.

TIP

It may appear that you have too much stuffing when you first tie the pork. But once all the strings are in place, it's easy to enclose the meat completely around the fruit mixture.

Preheat oven to 350° F (180° C)
Roasting pan with rack

Stuffing:

1 tbsp	butter	15 mL
1/3 cup	chopped green onions	75 mL
1 tsp	ground cumin	5 mL
1/2 tsp	curry powder	2 mL
1 cup	chopped mixed dried fruits, such as apricots, prunes, apples, cranberries	250 mL
1/2 cup	soft bread crumbs	125 mL
1 tsp	grated orange rind	5 mL
1	egg, beaten	1
	Salt and pepper	
3 lbs	boneless pork loin roast	1.5 kg
2 tsp	vegetable oil	10 mL
1	large clove garlic, minced	1
1 tsp	rubbed sage	5 mL
1/2 tsp	dried thyme	25 mL
1 tbsp	all-purpose flour	15 mL
1/2 cup	white wine *or* chicken stock	125 mL
3/4 cup	chicken stock	175 mL

1. In a small skillet, melt butter over medium heat. Add green onions, cumin and curry powder; cook, stirring, for 2 minutes or until softened.

2. In a bowl combine onion mixture, dried fruits, bread crumbs, orange rind and egg; season with salt and pepper.

3. Remove strings from pork roast; unfold roast and trim excess fat. Place pork roast, boned side up, on work surface. Cover with plastic wrap and pound using a meat mallet to flatten slightly. Season with salt and pepper; spread stuffing down center of meat. Roll the pork around the stuffing and tie securely at 6 intervals with butcher's string.

4. Place roast on rack in roasting pan. In a small bowl, combine oil, garlic, sage and thyme; spread over pork roast and season with salt and pepper.

5. Roast in preheated oven for 1 1/2 to 1 3/4 hours or until meat thermometer registers 160° F (70° C).

6. Remove roast to cutting board; tent with foil and let stand for 10 minutes before carving.

7. Pour off fat in pan. Place over medium heat; sprinkle with flour. Cook, stirring, for 1 minute or until lightly colored. Add wine, if using; cook until partially reduced. Add stock and bring to a boil, scraping any brown bits from bottom of pan. Season with salt and pepper to taste. Strain sauce through a fine sieve into a warm sauceboat. Cut pork into thick slices and serve accompanied with gravy.

Spicy Lamb Stew

Serves 6

Sometimes you crave a dish that explodes with spicy flavors. The ginger and hot red pepper flakes used here will satisfy that craving — and soothe your soul, too. I like to serve this spice-infused stew with basmati rice.

TIP

How to cook basmati rice

Rinse 1 1/2 cups (375 mL) rice in several changes of cold water. Place in bowl; add cold water to cover. Let soak 15 minutes; drain. In a saucepan bring 2 1/4 cups (550 mL) water and 1 tbsp (15 mL) oil to a boil; add rice and 1 tsp (5 mL) salt. Return to boil, reduce heat to low and simmer, covered, for 10 minutes. Remove and let stand, covered, for 5 minutes. Uncover and fluff with a fork.

◆

Fresh coriander, also called cilantro or Chinese parsley, lasts only few days in the fridge before it deteriorates and turns tasteless. Wash coriander well, spin dry and wrap in paper towels; store in plastic bag in the fridge. Leave the roots on — they keep the leaves fresh.

◆

Buy a 3-lb (1.5 kg) leg of lamb or shoulder roast to get 1 1/2 lbs (750 g) boneless lamb. Beef can be substituted for the lamb; increase cooking time to 1 1/2 hours or until meat is tender.

2 tbsp	vegetable oil (approximate)	25 mL
1 1/2 lbs	boneless lean lamb, cut into 1-inch (2.5 cm) cubes	750 g
1	large onion, chopped	1
2	cloves garlic, finely chopped	2
1 tbsp	minced ginger root	15 mL
1 tsp	ground cumin	5 mL
1 tsp	ground coriander	5 mL
1/2 tsp	cinnamon	2 mL
1/2 tsp	salt	2 mL
1/4 tsp	red pepper flakes (or more, to taste)	1 mL
Pinch	ground cloves	Pinch
1 tbsp	all-purpose flour	15 mL
1/2 cup	plain yogurt	125 mL
1	large tomato, chopped	1
1/2 cup	lamb stock *or* chicken stock	125 mL
1/4 cup	chopped fresh coriander *or* parsley	50 mL

1. In a large saucepan, heat 1 tbsp (15 mL) of the oil over medium-high heat; cook lamb in batches, adding more oil as needed, until browned on all sides. Remove from pan and set aside.

2. Reduce heat to medium. Add onion, garlic, ginger root, cumin, coriander, cinnamon, salt, red pepper flakes and cloves; cook, stirring, for 2 minutes or until softened.

3. Sprinkle with flour; stir in yogurt. Cook for 1 minute or until thickened. Add lamb with any accumulated juices, tomato and stock; bring to a boil. Reduce heat and simmer, covered, for 45 minutes or until lamb is tender. Sprinkle with coriander or parsley before serving.

Zesty Barbecued Spareribs

Serves 4

"You've got to put your rib recipe in your cookbook," advised my teenage son, whose favorite dinner request is a plate of these succulent ribs. So here it is. And since the only way to eat ribs is with your fingers, be sure to have plenty of napkins handy.

TIP

Ribs are great on the barbecue, too. Partially cook ribs in oven for 45 minutes as directed in recipe. Complete cooking on grill over medium-low flame, basting often with the sauce.

◆

Tabasco is the most familiar brand of hot sauce, so we've used it here. But supermarket shelves now boast a large assortment of hot sauces — some quite mild, others having a fiery kick — so experiment with various sauces available and add according to taste.

Preheat oven to 375° (190° C)
Shallow roasting pan or broiler pan, with rack

3 to 4 lbs	pork spareribs	1.5 to 2 kg
	Salt and pepper	
1 cup	prepared chili sauce *or* ketchup	250 mL
1/2 cup	honey	125 mL
1	small onion, finely chopped	1
2	cloves garlic, minced	2
2 tbsp	Worcestershire sauce	25 mL
2 tbsp	lemon juice	25 mL
1 tbsp	Dijon mustard	15 mL
1 tsp	Tabasco or other hot pepper sauce, or to taste	5 mL
1	lemon, cut into wedges	1

1. Place ribs on rack in roasting pan; season with salt and pepper. Cover with foil. Roast in preheated oven for 45 minutes.

2. In a small saucepan, combine chili sauce, honey, onion, garlic, Worcestershire sauce, lemon juice, mustard and Tabasco sauce. Bring to a boil; reduce heat and simmer, stirring occasionally, for 10 to 15 minutes or until slightly thickened.

3. Remove foil; brush ribs generously on both sides with sauce. Roast, uncovered, for 45 minutes, brushing generously every 15 minutes with the sauce, until spareribs are nicely glazed and tender.

4. Cut into serving portions; serve with any remaining sauce and lemon wedges.

Bistro Lentils with Smoked Sausage

Serves 6

It's Friday night. You've worked hard all week. Don't even bother setting the table. Here's a supper dish that's easy to balance on your lap while you relax in front of the TV set. As an added bonus, this dish goes great with a cold beer.

Any kind of smoked sausage or ham works well. The smaller-sized green Laird lentils hold their shape in cooking and are the kind I prefer for this recipe.

3 1/2 cups	chicken stock *or* vegetable stock (approximate)	875 mL
1 1/2 cups	lentils, picked over and rinsed	375 mL
1/2 tsp	dried thyme	2 mL
2 tbsp	olive oil	25 mL
1 cup	diced red onions	250 mL
3	cloves garlic, finely chopped	3
2	carrots, peeled and diced	2
1 cup	diced fennel *or* celery	250 mL
1	sweet red pepper, diced	1
2 tbsp	balsamic vinegar	25 mL
8 oz	smoked sausage, such as kielbasa, cut into 1/2-inch (1 cm) chunks	250 g
	Pepper	
1/4 cup	chopped fresh parsley	50 mL

1. In a large saucepan, bring stock to a boil over high heat. Add lentils and thyme; reduce heat to medium-low, cover and simmer for 25 to 30 minutes or until lentils are just tender but still hold their shape.

2. Meanwhile, heat oil in a large nonstick skillet over medium heat. Add onions, garlic, carrots and fennel; cook, stirring often, for 8 minutes. Add red pepper; cook, stirring, for 2 minutes more or until vegetables are just tender. Stir in vinegar; remove from heat.

3. Add vegetables and smoked sausage to lentils in saucepan; season with pepper to taste. Cover and cook for 5 to 8 minutes more or until sausage is heated through. (Add more stock or water, if necessary, to prevent lentils from sticking.) Stir in parsley. Serve warm or at room temperature.

Veal Paprikash

Serves 4

We've somehow forgotten this delicious classic preparation — and it's worth considering again. Together, the golden red paprika and tangy sour cream bring out the best in tender veal and meaty mushrooms.

TIP

Fettuccine or broad egg noodles make a delicious companion to this creamy veal in mushroom sauce.

◆

The most flavorful paprika comes from Hungary where it ranges in strength from mild (sweet) to hot.

2 tbsp	vegetable oil	25 mL
1 lb	grain-fed veal scallops *or* boneless beef sirloin, cut into thin strips	500 g
4 cups	quartered mushrooms (about 12 oz [375 g])	1 L
1	large onion, halved lengthwise and thinly sliced	1
2	cloves garlic, minced	2
4 tsp	sweet Hungarian paprika	20 mL
1/2 tsp	dried marjoram	2 mL
1/2 tsp	salt	2 mL
1/4 tsp	pepper	1 mL
1 tbsp	all-purpose flour	15 mL
3/4 cup	chicken stock	175 mL
1/2 cup	sour cream	125 mL
	Salt and pepper	

1. In a large nonstick skillet, heat half the oil over high heat; stir-fry veal in 2 batches, each for 3 minutes or until browned but still pink inside. Transfer to a plate along with pan juices; keep warm.

2. Reduce heat to medium. Add remaining oil. Add mushrooms, onion, garlic, paprika, marjoram, salt and pepper; cook, stirring often, for 7 minutes or until lightly colored.

3. Sprinkle mushroom mixture with flour; pour in stock. Cook, stirring, for 2 minutes or until thickened. Stir in sour cream. Return veal and accumulated juices to pan; cook 1 minute more or until heated through. Adjust seasoning with salt and pepper to taste; serve immediately.

Veal Ragout With Sweet Peppers

Serves 8

I like to make this delicious comfort stew ahead and have it tucked away in the freezer ready for company. Adding the peppers at the end of cooking helps keep their shape and lends a slightly smoky taste that lingers in your memory long after the last bite.

TIP

Use a combination of green, red and yellow peppers for maximum color effect.

◆

Beef can be substituted for the veal. Serve with SAFFRON RICE PILAF (see variation to recipe for HERBED RICE PILAF, page 115).

4 tbsp	olive oil (approximate)	60 mL
3 lbs	lean boneless veal, cut into 1-inch (2.5 cm) cubes	1.5 kg
2 tbsp	all-purpose flour	25 mL
1	Spanish onion (about 1 lb [500 g]), chopped	1
4	large cloves garlic, finely chopped	4
1 tsp	dried thyme	5 mL
1 tsp	paprika	5 mL
1	bay leaf	1
1 tsp	salt	5 mL
1/2 tsp	pepper	2 mL
1 cup	red wine *or* beef stock	250 mL
4	tomatoes, chopped	4
4	sweet peppers (any color), cubed	4
1/3 cup	chopped fresh parsley	75 mL

1. In a bowl toss veal cubes with flour until well-coated. In a Dutch oven or large heavy saucepan, heat 1 tbsp (15 mL) of the oil over high heat. In small batches, add veal and cook until nicely browned on all sides, adding more oil as needed. Remove and set aside.

2. Reduce heat to medium. Add 1 tbsp (15 mL) more oil. Add onion, garlic, thyme, paprika, bay leaf, salt and pepper; cook, stirring often, for 5 minutes or until softened.

3. Add wine or stock and bring to a boil. Stir in veal along with accumulated juices; add tomatoes. Bring to boil; reduce heat to medium-low and simmer, covered, for 1 1/4 to 1 1/2 hours or until veal is tender. (The recipe can be prepared to this point up to 48 hours ahead, then covered and refrigerated — or freeze for up to 3 months. Before reheating, let defrost in fridge overnight. Bring to a boil; cover and simmer for 20 minutes or until veal is thoroughly heated.)

How to freeze (and reheat) soups and casseroles

Label and date containers and casseroles before refrigerating or freezing.

◆

Meat- and chicken-based soups, stews and casseroles can be kept safely for up to 3 days in the refrigerator; vegetable-based dishes can be kept refrigerated for 5 days.

◆

To reheat, place in saucepan over medium heat, stirring occasionally, until piping hot;
or
place in covered casserole and bake in 350° F (180° C) oven for 30 to 45 minutes or until piping hot;
or
microwave, covered with lid or microwave-safe plastic wrap, at Medium-High for 9 to 15 minutes, stirring occasionally, or until heated through to center.

For single servings, microwave, covered, at Medium-High for 3 to 5 minutes.

◆

Stews, soups and casseroles can be frozen for up to 3 months. Defrost in refrigerator overnight and reheat as directed above.

4. Shortly before serving, heat 1 tbsp (15 mL) oil in a large nonstick skillet over high heat; cook pepper cubes, stirring, for 2 to 3 minutes or until lightly colored. Reduce heat to medium-low, cover and simmer for 8 to 10 minutes or until tender-crisp.

5. Add peppers to veal; stir in parsley and simmer for 5 minutes to let the flavors blend. Adjust seasoning with salt and pepper to taste. Remove bay leaf.

Quebec Meat Pie (Tourtiere)

Serves 6

There are many versions of Quebec's famous meat pie. This exceptional one from my friend Helene Laurendeau is drawn from both her mother and mother-in-law's recipes. These, in turn, came from the late Jehane Benoit, the doyenne of French Canadian cooking. Helene often prepares individual meat pies for easy serving when her family gathers for Christmas dinner.

TIP

Unbaked meat pies freeze well for up to 2 months. Let defrost in refrigerator overnight before baking.

Preheat oven to 425° F (220° C)
9-inch (23 cm) pie plate, lightly greased

Filling:

1 lb	lean ground pork	500 g
8 oz	lean ground veal	250 g
1	large onion, finely chopped	1
2	cloves garlic, minced	2
3/4 tsp	dried savory	4 mL
3/4 tsp	salt	4 mL
1/4 tsp	ground allspice	1 mL
1/4 tsp	ground cloves	1 mL
1/4 tsp	pepper	1 mL
3/4 cup	water	175 mL
1/3 cup	dry bread crumbs	75 mL
	Pastry for double crust 9-inch (23 cm) pie (see recipe, facing page)	
1	egg yolk	1

1. In a Dutch oven or large saucepan over medium-high heat, cook pork and veal, crushing with the back of a spoon, for 5 minutes. Add onion, garlic, savory, salt, allspice, cloves and pepper; cook, stirring often, for 5 minutes.

2. Add water; bring to a boil. Reduce heat; partially cover and simmer, stirring occasionally, for 20 minutes or until most of liquid has evaporated. Remove from heat. Stir in bread crumbs to absorb excess moisture; let cool, then refrigerate until chilled.

3. Meanwhile, line prepared pie plate with pastry. Trim edges. Spoon filling into pie shell. Cover with top pastry; trim edges, crimp to seal and cut steam vents. In a small bowl, beat egg yolk with 2 tsp (10 mL) water. Brush pastry with egg wash.

4. Bake pie in preheated oven for 15 minutes; reduce heat to 375° (190° C) and bake for 25 to 30 minutes more or until pastry is golden.

Makes enough pastry for 9-inch (23 cm) double crust pie

ALL-PURPOSE PIE PASTRY

1/2 cup	cold butter, cubed	125 mL
1/4 cup	shortening	50 mL
2 cups	all-purpose flour	500 mL
1/4 tsp	salt	1 mL
5 to 6 tbsp	cold water	75 to 90 mL

1. Place butter and shortening on a plate; place in freezer for 20 minutes or until firm. Cut into small bits.

2. In a food processor combine flour and salt. Add butter and shortening; process to make fine crumbs. Transfer mixture to a bowl; sprinkle with water and toss. Gather dough into a ball.

3. Divide dough in two. Shape each piece into a 5-inch (13 cm) disc; wrap in plastic wrap. Refrigerate for 1 hour before using.

Jambalaya

Serves 6 to 8

Jambalaya is the perfect party dish. A one-pot wonder originating from New Orleans, it pleases all palates with its piquant flavors and mix of chicken, sausage and shrimp. Set this dish on the table and watch it disappear.

Try not to stir the jambalaya or the rice will turn sticky.

◆

Try replacing the sausage with 8 oz (250 g) cubed smoked ham.

◆

If using chicken thighs with the bone in, increase cooking time by 5 to 10 minutes.

Preheat oven to 350° F (180° C)
12-cup (3 L) baking dish or ovenproof serving dish

2 tbsp	olive oil	25 mL
1 1/2 lbs	skinless, boneless chicken thighs (about 10 to 12)	750 g
1/2 lb	andouille, chorizo or other spicy smoked sausage, cut into 1/4-inch (5 mm) slices	250 g
1	large onion, chopped	1
3	cloves garlic, finely chopped	3
2	stalks celery, diced	2
1	sweet green pepper, diced	1
1	sweet red pepper, diced	1
1 tsp	dried thyme	5 mL
1 tsp	paprika	5 mL
1/2 tsp	salt	2 mL
1/4 tsp	ground allspice	1 mL
1/4 tsp	cayenne pepper	1 mL
1 1/2 cups	long grain rice	375 mL
1	can (14 oz [398 mL]) tomatoes, chopped, with juice	1
1 3/4 cups	chicken stock	425 mL
8 oz	medium raw shrimp, in the shell	250 g
1/3 cup	chopped fresh parsley	75 mL
3	green onions, finely chopped	3

1. In a Dutch oven, heat oil over medium-high heat. Add chicken and cook for 5 minutes or until browned on both sides. Remove to plate.

2. Add sausage, onion, garlic, celery, green and red peppers, thyme, paprika, salt, allspice and cayenne pepper; cook, stirring often, for 5 minutes or until vegetables are softened. Return chicken to dish along with accumulated juices. (The recipe can be prepared ahead up to this point; let cool, cover and refrigerate.)

3. Stir in rice, tomatoes with juice and stock; bring to a boil. Transfer to baking dish. Cover and bake in preheated oven for 30 minutes or until rice and chicken are just tender.

4. Stir in shrimp, parsley and green onions; cover and bake 5 to 8 minutes longer or until shrimp turns pink.

Seafood Supreme

Do you pine for the days when elegant luncheons were in fashion? Here's a special dish reminiscent of days gone by, when ladies in white gloves lunched ever so elegantly on richly flavored seafood sauces served in puff pastry shells. You could serve this dish the same way, or serve it over rice, or toss with pasta.

TIP

Cooked lobster can replace part of the shellfish.

◆

For a less expensive version, omit scallops and shrimp; increase the amount of sole, haddock or cod to 1 1/2 lbs (750 g).

◆

The moisture content of fresh and frozen seafood differs and may result in the finished sauce being too thick or too thin. To eliminate this problem, poach the uncooked seafood first in wine and stock.

1 cup	fish stock *or* chicken stock (approximate)	250 mL
1/2 cup	dry white wine or vermouth	125 mL
8 oz	sole or other white fish, cut into 1-inch (2.5 cm) cubes	250 g
1/2 lb	small scallops	250 g
1/2 lb	small cooked, peeled shrimp	250 g
3 tbsp	butter	45 mL
1/3 cup	finely chopped green onions	75 mL
3/4 cup	diced sweet red peppers	175 mL
1/4 cup	all-purpose flour	50 mL
1/2 cup	whipping (35%) cream	125 mL
	Salt and white pepper	
2 tbsp	chopped fresh dill *or* parsley	25 mL

1. In a saucepan bring stock and wine to a boil over medium heat. Add sole cubes; poach 2 minutes (start timing when fish is added to stock). Add scallops; poach 1 to 2 minutes more or until seafood is opaque. Remove using a slotted spoon; place in a bowl along with shrimp and set aside.

2. Strain stock into glass measure; there should be 2 cups (500 mL). Add water, if necessary; reserve.

3. In a saucepan melt butter over medium heat. Add onions and red peppers; cook, stirring, for 3 minutes or until softened. Blend in flour; pour in reserved stock mixture. Bring to a boil, stirring, until sauce is very thick and smooth. Stir in cream; bring to a boil.

4. Just before serving, add seafood and heat through. Season with salt and white pepper to taste; stir in dill or parsley. Serve immediately.

Leek and Halibut Ragout

Serves 6

Fish a comfort food?
You bet — particularly in this
warming stew, where the fish
is paired with wonderful veggies. Never mind that it fits in
perfectly with today's healthy
lifestyle. It's still a classic
comfort dish.

TIP

Don't overcook the
vegetables in this main course
dish; they should still retain
their bright color and texture.

◆

Saffron makes this stew
special; you can, however,
eliminate the saffron and
substitute chopped fresh dill
for the parsley.

2 tbsp	olive oil	25 mL
2	medium leeks, white and light green part only, chopped	2
2	cloves garlic, finely chopped	2
2 tbsp	all-purpose flour	25 mL
2 1/2 cups	fish stock *or* chicken stock	625 mL
1/2 cup	white wine *or* additional stock	125 mL
1/4 tsp	saffron threads, crushed	1 mL
2 cups	diced peeled potatoes	500 mL
2	medium carrots, peeled and diagonally sliced	2
2	small zucchini, halved lengthwise and sliced	2
1	small sweet red pepper, diced	1
1 1/2 lbs	halibut, trimmed and cut into 1-inch (2.5 cm) cubes	750 g
	Salt and pepper	
1/4 cup	chopped fresh parsley	50 mL

1. In a large saucepan, heat oil over medium heat; add leeks and garlic; cook, stirring often, for 5 minutes or until tender. (Do not let leeks brown.)

2. Stir in flour; add stock, wine and saffron. Bring to a boil, stirring, until thickened. Add potatoes and carrots; reduce heat to medium-low and simmer, covered, for 15 minutes. Stir in zucchini and red pepper; cook 5 minutes more or until vegetables are just tender.

3. Add halibut; cook for 3 to 5 minutes more or until fish is opaque. Adjust seasoning with salt and pepper to taste. Sprinkle with parsley; ladle into warmed wide shallow bowls.

Salmon with Lemon-Ginger Sauce

Serves 4

Fresh ginger root gives such a sparkling flavor to salmon — or any fish, for that matter. Substituting dried ground ginger just doesn't come close to imparting the same crisp taste as fresh ginger root, which is available in most supermarkets and produce stores.

TIP

To store ginger root, peel it, place in glass jar and add white wine or sherry to cover. As an added bonus, you can use the ginger-infused wine or sherry to flavor other fish or chicken dishes, or stir-fries.

◆

One of the best uses for the microwave in my kitchen is for quickly cooking fish such as this salmon.

◆

Arrange fish and sauce in a shallow baking dish and cover with microwave-safe plastic wrap; turn back one corner to vent. Microwave at Medium for 4 minutes. Turn fish over and re-cover; microwave at Medium for 3 to 5 minutes more or until salmon turns opaque.

◆

This fish dish is also great to cook on the barbecue.

Preheat oven to 425° F (220° C)

4	salmon fillets, 5 oz (150 g) each	4

Marinade:

2	green onions	2
1 1/2 tsp	minced fresh ginger root	7 mL
1	clove garlic, minced	1
2 tbsp	soya sauce	25 mL
1 tbsp	fresh lemon juice	15 mL
1 tsp	grated lemon rind	5 mL
1 tsp	granulated sugar	5 mL
1 tsp	sesame oil	5 mL

1. Chop green onions; set aside chopped green tops for garnish. In a bowl combine white part of onions, ginger root, garlic, soya sauce, lemon juice and rind, sugar and sesame oil.

2. Place salmon fillets in a single layer in a shallow baking dish. Pour marinade over; let stand at room temperature for 15 minutes or in the refrigerator for up to 1 hour.

3. Bake, uncovered, in preheated oven for 13 to 15 minutes or until salmon turns opaque. Arrange on serving plates, spoon sauce over and sprinkle with green onion tops.

Cod Provençal

Serves 4

What to do with fresh cod from the market and ripe tomatoes plucked from your garden? Add some briny olives and pungent capers, and make this delicious fish dish that bursts with the sunny flavors of the Mediterranean.

TIP

Don't skimp on the olive oil — it's what gives this dish its distinct character and flavor.

Preheat oven to 425° F (220° C)
Shallow baking dish

1 1/4 lbs	cod *or* halibut, cut into 4 pieces	625 g
	Salt and pepper	
2	ripe tomatoes, diced	2
2	green onions	2
1	clove garlic, minced	1
1/4 cup	Kalamata olives, rinsed, cut into slivers	50 mL
2 tbsp	chopped fresh parsley *or* basil	25 mL
1 tbsp	capers, rinsed and drained	15 mL
Pinch	red pepper flakes (optional)	Pinch
2 tbsp	olive oil	25 mL

1. Arrange cod in a single layer in baking dish. Season with salt and pepper.

2. In a bowl combine tomatoes, onions, garlic, olives, parsley, capers and hot pepper flakes, if using; season with salt and pepper. Spoon tomato-olive mixture over fish fillets; drizzle with oil.

3. Bake in preheated oven for 15 to 20 minutes or until fish flakes when tested with a fork. Serve in warmed wide shallow bowls and spoon pan juices over.

sole fillets with vibrant red pepper stuffing, napped in a light wine and cream sauce. It makes an attractive fish dish that never fails to impress.

In the past, fish dishes were adorned with silky rich sauces loaded with cream and butter. Adding only a small amount of whipping cream still gives this sauce its luxurious and creamy appeal, but keeps the calorie count way down.

Stuffed Sole

Preheat oven to 425° F (220° C)
9-inch (2.5 L) square baking dish

1 tbsp	butter	15 mL
1/4 cup	chopped green onions	50 mL
1 cup	chopped mushrooms	250 mL
1	sweet red pepper, cut into very thin 1-inch (2.5 cm) strips	1
1 tsp	dried tarragon	5 mL
	Salt and white pepper	
8	small sole fillets (about 1 1/2 pounds [750 g])	8
1/3 cup	white wine *or* fish stock	75 mL
2 tsp	cornstarch	10 mL
1 tbsp	cold water	15 mL
1/3 cup	whipping (35%) cream	75 mL

1. In a nonstick skillet, heat butter over medium heat. Add onions, mushrooms, pepper and tarragon; cook, stirring, for 3 minutes or until softened. Let cool.

2. Lay sole fillets, skinned side down, on work surface with smaller tapered ends closest to you; season with salt and pepper. Spoon a generous tablespoonful (15 to 17 mL) on bottom ends of fillets. Roll up and place fillets seam-side down in baking dish. Pour wine or stock over. (Recipe can be prepared up to this point earlier in day, then covered and refrigerated.)

3. To bake, cover with lid or foil; place in preheated oven for 16 to 20 minutes or until fish turns opaque.

4. Using a slotted spoon, remove fillets and arrange on serving plate; cover and keep warm.

5. Strain fish juices through a fine sieve into a medium saucepan; bring to a boil over high heat and reduce to about 1/2 cup (125 mL). In a glass measure, blend cornstarch with water; stir in cream. Pour into saucepan, whisking constantly, until sauce comes to a boil and thickens. Adjust seasoning with salt and pepper to taste. Spoon sauce over fish and serve.

EASY COOKING

Beef-Stuffed Spuds

Serves 4

Baked potatoes stuffed with a variety of fillings is a popular meal in my house. I make them ahead for those nights when everyone is on a different schedule. The potatoes need only a quick reheat in the microwave as each person walks through the door for an instant supper.

TIP

How to bake potatoes
Scrub baking potatoes (10 oz [300 g] each) well and pierce skins with a fork in several places to allow steam to escape.

To oven bake: Place in 400° F (200° C) oven for 1 hour or until potatoes give slightly when squeezed.

To microwave: Arrange potatoes in a circle, spacing 1-inch (2.5 cm) apart on roasting rack or on a paper towel in microwave oven. Microwave at High, turning over halfway through cooking, until potatoes are just tender when pierced with a skewer.

Microwave cooking times at High: 1 potato, 4 to 5 minutes; 2 potatoes, 6 to 8 minutes; 4 potatoes, 10 to 12 minutes

◆

For moist potatoes wrap cooked potatoes individually in foil. For drier potatoes, wrap in a dry towel. Let stand 5 minutes.

Preheat oven to 400° F (200° C)
Shallow baking dish

4	large potatoes (about 10 oz [300 g] each)	4
8 oz	lean ground beef *or* ground veal	250 g
1/3 cup	finely chopped onions	75 mL
1	clove garlic, minced	1
1 tsp	Worcestershire sauce	5 mL
	Salt and pepper	
1/2 cup	sour cream *or* plain yogurt *or* buttermilk (approximate)	125 mL
1 cup	shredded Cheddar cheese	250 mL
2 tbsp	chopped parsley	25 mL

1. Bake or microwave potatoes as directed (see Tip, at left).

2. In a large nonstick skillet over medium-high heat, cook beef, breaking up with back of spoon, for 4 minutes or until no longer pink.

3. Reduce heat to medium. Add onions, garlic and Worcestershire sauce; season with salt and pepper. Cook, stirring often, for 4 minutes or until onions are softened.

4. Cut warm potatoes in half lengthwise. Carefully scoop out each potato, leaving a 1/4-inch (5 mm) shell; set shells aside.

5. In a bowl mash potatoes with potato masher or fork; beat in enough sour cream until smooth. Stir in beef mixture, half the cheese and all the parsley; season with salt and pepper to taste. Spoon into potato shells; top with remaining cheese.

6. Arrange in shallow baking dish; bake in preheated oven for 15 minutes or until cheese is melted. Or place on microwave-safe rack or large serving plate; microwave at Medium-High for 5 to 7 minutes or until heated through and cheese melts.

Broccoli and Cheese-Stuffed Potatoes

Serves 4

These delicious baked potatoes are great to pack along to work if you have the use of a microwave for reheating.

TIP

Cheddar and broccoli are a classic combo, but get adventurous with whatever cheese and vegetables are in the fridge. Another favorite is mozzarella cheese and lightly sautéed mushrooms and diced red peppers seasoned with basil.

Preheat oven to 400° F (200° C)
Shallow baking dish

4	large baking potatoes (about 10 oz [300 g] each)	4
3 cups	small broccoli florets and peeled, chopped stems	750 mL
1/2 cup	sour cream *or* plain yogurt *or* buttermilk (approximate)	125 mL
2	green onions, chopped	2
1 1/3 cups	shredded Cheddar *or* Gruyere cheese	325 mL
	Salt and cayenne pepper	

1. Bake or microwave potatoes as directed (see Tip, page 84).

2. In a saucepan cook or steam broccoli until just crisp-tender. (Or place in covered casserole and microwave at High for 3 minutes.) Drain well.

3. Cut a thin slice from tops of warm potatoes. Scoop out potato leaving a 1/4-inch (5 mm) shell, being careful not to tear the skins.

4. In a bowl mash potato with potato masher or fork; beat in enough sour cream until smooth. Add broccoli, onion and 1 cup (250 mL) of the cheese. Season with salt and a dash of cayenne pepper to taste.

5. Spoon filling into potato shells, mounding the tops. Arrange in shallow baking dish; sprinkle with remaining cheese. Bake in preheated oven for 20 minutes or until cheese melts. Or place on a rack and microwave at Medium-High for 5 to 7 minutes or until heated through and cheese melts.

Mu Shu-Style Pork

Serves 4

When my family craves Chinese take-out, that's when I turn to this recipe. The name *Mu Shu* may sound exotic, but it's really an easy stir-fry served in a wrapper that's fun to eat. Here, flour tortillas replace thin Mandarin pancakes in this streamlined Chinese dish.

TIP

I always keep flour tortillas on hand, as they make versatile sandwich wrappers for all kinds of fillings. To warm the tortillas, wrap in foil and place in 350° F (180° C) oven for 20 minutes. Or wrap 4 at a time in paper towels and microwave at Medium-High for about 1 1/2 minutes.

◆

Make this recipe with boneless chicken breasts (or beef, such as sirloin) instead of pork.

◆

Use whatever vegetables you have in the fridge. Try zucchini, snow peas or celery. The actual cooking takes only a few minutes, so be sure to have all the ingredients assembled before you start.

1 tbsp	vegetable oil	15 mL
2 tsp	minced ginger root	10 mL
1	large clove garlic, minced	1
12 oz	lean boneless pork loin, cut into thin strips	375 g
1/4 cup	water	50 mL
1 cup	carrots, peeled and cut into thin diagonal slices	250 mL
2 cups	small broccoli florets and chopped, peeled stems	500 mL
1	sweet red pepper, cut into thin strips, 1 1/2 inches (4 cm) long	1
2 tbsp	soya sauce	25 mL
	Hot pepper sauce to taste	
2 tsp	cornstarch	10 mL
2 to 4 tbsp	hoisin sauce (approximate)	25 to 50 mL
8	warm flour tortillas (8-inch [20 cm] size)	8

1. In a large nonstick skillet or wok, heat oil over high heat. Add ginger root and garlic; cook, stirring, for 15 seconds, or until fragrant. Add pork; cook, stirring, for 3 minutes or until no longer pink. Transfer to a plate.

2. Add water and carrots to skillet; cover and cook 1 minute. Add broccoli and red pepper; cover and cook 2 minutes more or until vegetables are crisp-tender.

3. In bowl, blend soya sauce, cornstarch and hot pepper sauce until smooth. Return pork to skillet; pour in soya sauce mixture. Cook, stirring, for 1 minute or until sauce thickens.

4. Spread each tortilla with 1 to 2 tsp (5 to 10 mL) hoisin sauce; add about 1/2 cup (125 mL) pork mixture. Fold 1-inch (2.5 cm) of the tortilla along one side over filling; roll up starting at side closest to you to enclose filling. Serve immediately.

Hot Beef Subs

Serves 4

When my kids were young, their idea of a night out was a trip to MacDonald's. Now in their teens, they prefer the fast food offered by sandwich shops. This recipe is my response when the sandwich craving strikes.

TIP

I always grill extra flank or round steak when barbecuing, so I have leftovers to make these terrific sandwiches for next night's supper. It's also a nifty way to deal with leftovers from Sunday's beef roast. In a pinch, deli roast beef from the supermarket also works well.

4	crusty submarine rolls	4
1/4 cup	light cream cheese, softened	50 mL
2 tbsp	mayonnaise	25 mL
2 tbsp	Dijon mustard	25 mL
2	tomatoes, thinly sliced	2
1 tbsp	olive oil	15 mL
1	small red onion, thinly sliced	1
1	large clove garlic, minced	1
1 cup	sliced mushrooms	250 mL
Half	large sweet green pepper, cut into thin 1 1/2 inches (4 cm) strips	Half
1/2 tsp	dried oregano	2 mL
1 cup	thin strips cooked flank steak *or* round steak	250 mL
	Salt and pepper	

1. Split rolls along 1 side and open; grill or broil cut sides until toasted.

2. In a bowl, blend cream cheese, mayonnaise and mustard; spread over cut sides of rolls. Line with tomato slices. Set aside.

3. In a large nonstick skillet, heat oil over medium-high heat. Add onion, garlic, mushrooms, green pepper and oregano; cook, stirring often, for 3 to 5 minutes.

4. Add beef; cook, stirring, for 1 minute more or until hot. Season with salt and pepper to taste. Spoon into rolls; serve immediately.

Yummy Parmesan Chicken Fingers

Serves 4

What a relief to know when you come home frazzled from a day at work, you can count on these tasty chicken fingers stashed away in your freezer. Round out the meal with rice and a steamed vegetable (like broccoli) for a dinner that's on the table in 30 minutes.

TIP

Buy boneless chicken breasts when they're featured as a supermarket special and make batches of chicken fingers to freeze ahead. Use fresh (not defrosted) chicken breasts; prepare recipe as directed, placing unbaked strips on a rack set on baking sheet. Freeze until firm; transfer to a storage container. Can be frozen for up to 2 months. No need to defrost before baking.

◆

You can also make extra batches of the crumb mixture and store in the freezer.

◆

Instead of boneless chicken breasts, prepare skinless chicken drumsticks in the same way but bake in a 375° F (190° C) oven for 35 to 40 minutes or until tender. The butter baste gives a nice flavor, but is optional if counting calories.

Preheat oven to 400° F (200° C)
Baking sheet

1/2 cup	finely crushed soda cracker crumbs (about 16 crackers)	125 mL
1/3 cup	freshly grated Parmesan cheese	75 mL
1/2 tsp	dried basil	2 mL
1/2 tsp	dried marjoram	2 mL
1/2 tsp	paprika	2 mL
1/2 tsp	salt	2 mL
1/4 tsp	pepper	1 mL
4	skinless, boneless chicken breasts	4
1/3 cup	sour cream *or* plain yogurt (*or* 1 large egg, beaten)	75 mL
1	clove garlic, minced	1
2 tbsp	melted butter (optional)	25 mL

1. In a food processor combine cracker crumbs, Parmesan cheese, basil, marjoram, paprika, salt and pepper. Process to make fine crumbs. Place in shallow bowl.

2. Cut chicken breasts into 4 strips each. Place in a bowl; stir in sour cream and garlic. Using a fork, dip chicken strips in crumb mixture until evenly coated. Arrange on greased rack set on baking sheet. Brush tops lightly with melted butter, if desired.

3. Bake in preheated oven for 15 minutes or until no longer pink in center. (If frozen, bake for up to 25 minutes.)

Flatbread Pizzas

Serves 4

"Let's order pizza!" The next time you hear this request from your kids, assemble the ingredients here and get them cooking. Why order out when making pizza at home using store-bought bread bases and sauces is such a breeze? It's more economical, too.

TIP

This recipe is the perfect solution to deal with the odd bits of vegetables, cheese and deli left in my fridge by week's end. Vary the toppings according to what you have on hand including sliced pepperoni, chopped ham or broccoli.

◆

Four 7-inch (18 cm) pitas or 6 split English muffins can also be used. If necessary, arrange on 2 baking sheets; rotate halfway during baking so breads bake evenly. Reduce baking time to 10 minutes.

Preheat oven to 400° F (200° C)
Baking sheet

1 tbsp	vegetable oil *or* olive oil	15 mL
1	small onion, thinly sliced	1
1	clove garlic, minced	1
1 cup	sliced mushrooms	250 mL
1	small sweet green or red pepper, cut into thin strips	1
1/2 tsp	dried basil	2 mL
1/2 tsp	dried oregano	2 mL
1	12-inch (30 cm) prebaked pizza base *or* 9- by 12-inch (23 by 30 cm) focaccia	1
1/2 cup	store-bought pizza sauce (approximate)	125 mL
2 cups	shredded cheese, such as mozzarella, Fontina or provolone	500 mL

1. In a large nonstick skillet, heat oil over medium-high heat. Add onions, garlic, mushrooms, pepper, basil and oregano; cook, stirring, for 4 minutes or until softened.

2. Arrange pizza shell on baking sheet; spread with pizza sauce. Top with vegetables and shredded cheese.

3. Bake in preheated oven for 20 to 24 minutes or until cheese is melted.

Cheese and Salsa Quesadillas

Serves 4

Here's my modern rendition of grilled cheese: thin flour tortillas replace sliced bread, mozzarella substitutes for processed cheese and chunky salsa stands in for the ketchup. And the beans? They're optional, but make a wholesome addition.

TIP

I often serve these warm cheesy wedges with soup for an easy dinner. They're also great as a snack that both kids and grownups applaud.

◆

Use mild salsa to appease those with timid taste buds, but add a dash of hot pepper sauce to the filling for those who like a burst of heat.

1/2 cup	prepared salsa, plus additional for serving	125 mL
4	flour tortillas (8-inch [20 cm] size)	4
1 cup	canned black or pinto beans, rinsed and drained well	250 mL
1 cup	shredded mozzarella, Monterey Jack or Cheddar cheese	250 mL

1. Spread 2 tbsp (25 mL) salsa on one-half of each tortilla. Sprinkle with 1/4 cup (50 mL) each of the beans and the cheese. Fold tortillas over and press down lightly.

2. Heat a large nonstick skillet over medium heat; cook tortillas, 2 at a time, pressing down lightly with the back of a metal spatula, for about 2 minutes per side, until lightly toasted and cheese is melted. Or, place directly on barbecue grill over medium heat until lightly toasted on both sides.

3. Cut into wedges and serve warm with additional salsa, if desired.

Taco Pitas

Serves 4

Ever since I devised these yummy tacos, I walk right on by the prepackaged taco mixes and shells in supermarkets. Once the meat is browned, it takes no time to add the beans and seasonings to make the tasty filling. Aside from being lower in fat, I find pita breads make much better containers than taco shells, which tend to crumble when you bite into them and cause the filling to spill out.

◆

Double the recipe and freeze extras for another meal. The only major chore left to getting supper ready is shredding the cheese and preparing the vegetable garnishes — simple tasks that young cooks can handle.

TIP

To heat pitas, wrap in foil and place in a 350° F (180° C) oven for 15 to 20 minutes. Or wrap 4 at a time in paper towels and microwave at High for 1 to 1 1/2 minutes.

VARIATION

Sloppy Joe Pitas
Increase beef to 1 lb (500 g). Omit beans and add 1 can (7 1/2 oz [213 mL]) tomato sauce; cook 3 minutes more or until sauce is slightly thickened.

8 oz	lean ground beef	250 g
1	small onion, finely chopped	1
1	large garlic clove, minced	1
2 tsp	chili powder	10 mL
2 tsp	all-purpose flour	10 mL
1/2 tsp	dried oregano	2 mL
1/2 tsp	ground cumin	2 mL
Pinch	cayenne pepper	Pinch
1/2 cup	beef stock	125 mL
1	can (19 oz [540 mL]) pinto, black or red kidney beans, rinsed and drained	1
6	pitas (7-inch [18 cm] size), halved to form pockets, warmed	6
	Salsa, shredded lettuce, tomato wedges, pepper strips, shredded mozzarella or cheddar cheese	

1. In a large nonstick skillet over medium-high heat, cook beef, breaking up with the back of a spoon, for 4 minutes or until no longer pink.

2. Reduce heat to medium. Add onion, garlic, chili powder, flour, oregano, cumin and cayenne pepper. Cook, stirring often, for 5 minutes or until onions are softened.

3. Pour in stock; cook, stirring, until slightly thickened. Stir in beans; cook 2 minutes more or until heated through.

4. Spoon 1/4 cup (50 mL) of the mixture into pita pockets; top with salsa, lettuce, tomato, pepper and cheese.

Honey-Lemon Chicken Kabobs with Vegetable Rice

Serves 4

This easy family meal is a breeze to assemble and there are not many pots to bother with afterwards. A great short cut is to steam the vegetables in the rice for the last few minutes of cooking. The chicken is very versatile, too: grill it on the barbecue or under the broiler, or quickly stir-fry in a skillet.

TIP

Use vegetables such as sliced carrots, sliced celery, sliced halved zucchini, red pepper strips, small broccoli and cauliflower florets. Sliced carrots and celery take longer to cook so add along with rice to boiling stock.

◆

For convenience, you can use frozen vegetables here instead of fresh. Cook according to package directions on the stovetop or in the microwave oven; drain. Add to rice for the last 5 minutes of cooking to blend flavors.

Preheat broiler

2 cups	chicken stock	500 mL
1 cup	long-grain rice	250 mL
1 tsp	grated lemon rind	5 mL
3 cups	prepared vegetables (see Tip)	750 mL
4	boneless chicken breasts, cut into 1-inch (2.5 cm) cubes	4
1 tsp	dried oregano	5 mL
1 tbsp	honey	15 mL
1 tbsp	lemon juice	15 mL
1	garlic clove, minced	1
1/2 tsp	salt	2 mL
1 tbsp	olive oil	15 mL

1. Place 4 bamboo skewers in cold water to soak.

2. In a large saucepan, bring chicken stock to a boil; add rice and lemon rind. Reduce heat to low, cover and simmer for 15 minutes. Stir in vegetables; cover and cook 10 minutes more or until crisp-tender.

3. Meanwhile, in a bowl combine chicken, oregano, honey, lemon juice, garlic and salt. Let marinate at room temperature for 10 minutes.

4. Arrange oven rack 4 inches (10 cm) from broiler.

5. Thread chicken pieces on bamboo skewers; do not crowd. Arrange kabobs on wire rack set on baking sheet. Brush with oil. Place under preheated broiler; cook 4 to 5 minutes per side or until chicken is no longer pink. (Chicken pieces can also be cooked on the stovetop. Omit the bamboo skewers. Heat oil in a large nonstick skillet over medium-high heat; cook chicken, turning often, for 5 to 7 minutes or until no longer pink.)

6. To serve, divide rice mixture among serving plates and top with chicken.

Vegetable-Fried Rice

Serves 4

Use this recipe as a guide to create your own versions of fried rice, depending on what type of veggies you have in the fridge. With rice cooked ahead, it takes no time to prepare this quick supper dish.

TIP

Instead of peas, try substituting blanched diced carrots, snow peas cut into 1-inch (2.5 cm) pieces, 1 zucchini halved lengthwise and sliced, and small broccoli florets.

◆

To cook rice ahead
In a saucepan bring 2 cups (500 mL) water and 1/2 tsp (2 mL) salt to a boil; add 1 cup (250 mL) long-grain rice. Reduce heat; cover and simmer for 20 minutes or until rice is tender. Uncover, fluff with fork and let cool.

VARIATION

Chicken or Pork-Fried Rice
Cut 8 oz (250 g) chicken breasts or lean boneless pork loin into thin strips. In a skillet heat 1 tbsp (15 mL) oil over medium-high heat; cook meat, stirring, for 5 minutes or until no longer pink. Remove; keep warm. Continue with recipe as directed. Return meat to skillet with bean sprouts.

1 tbsp	vegetable oil	15 mL
3	green onions, chopped	3
1 1/2 tsp	minced ginger root	7 mL
1	clove garlic, minced	1
3 cups	cold cooked rice	750 mL
1 cup	frozen peas	250 mL
Half	sweet red pepper, cut into thin strips, 1 1/2 inches (4 cm) long	Half
2 cups	bean sprouts	500 mL
2 tbsp	soya sauce	25 mL
1 tsp	curry powder (optional)	5 mL

1. In a large nonstick skillet, heat oil over high heat. Add onions, ginger root and garlic; cook, stirring, for 15 seconds or until fragrant. Add rice and prepared vegetables; cook, stirring often, for 5 to 7 minutes or until rice is heated through and vegetables are tender.

2. In a small bowl, combine soya sauce and curry powder, if using; stir into rice mixture along with bean sprouts. Cook, stirring, for 1 to 2 minutes or until heated through. Serve immediately.

Ham and Potato Frittata

Serves 6

Nothing beats a delicious egg dish like this frittata for a special occasion breakfast or brunch, or for an easy supper dish. A frittata is an Italian version of an omelet. Unlike its finicky cousin, which needs careful flipping and turning, a frittata doesn't require any major cooking skills other than stirring — so it's almost impossible to ruin this dish.

TIP

Instead of ham, add 6 bacon slices, cooked until crisp and crumbled, to egg mixture.

◆

Bake or microwave 2 large potatoes the day before and refrigerate so cubes keep their shape during cooking.

Preheat oven to 375° F (190° C)

2 tbsp	butter	25 mL
1	small onion, finely chopped	1
2 cups	peeled cooked potatoes, cut into 1/2-inch (1 cm) cubes	500 mL
1	small sweet red pepper, finely diced (optional)	1
3/4 cup	diced smoked ham (about 4 oz [125 g])	175 mL
	Salt and pepper	
8	large eggs	8
2 tbsp	milk	25 mL
2 tbsp	finely chopped fresh parsley	25 mL
1 cup	shredded Cheddar, Edam or Havarti cheese	250 mL

1. In a large nonstick skillet, melt butter over medium-high heat. Add onion, potatoes, red pepper and ham; cook, stirring often, for 5 minutes or until vegetables are tender. Reduce heat to medium-low.

2. Meanwhile, in a large bowl, beat together eggs, milk and parsley; season with salt and pepper. Pour over potato mixture in skillet; cook, stirring gently, for about 1 minute, or until eggs start to set. (The eggs will appear semi-scrambled.) Stir in cheese.

3. If skillet handle is not ovenproof, wrap in double layer of aluminum foil to shield it from oven heat. Place in preheated oven for 15 to 20 minutes or until eggs are just set in center. Let cool 5 minutes. Turn out onto large serving plate and cut into wedges.

Turkey Fajitas

Serves 4

I love this recipe because it's a quick and easy main dish, yet it calls for only a few ingredients. It's ideal to serve when my children invite their friends over for an impromptu dinner. I set out bowls of the cheese, sour cream and salsa, and let everyone help themselves.

TIP

Turkey can also be barbecued: Marinate as directed and brush with 1 tbsp (15 mL) oil; grill over medium heat for 3 minutes per side or until no longer pink.

◆

To warm tortillas, wrap in foil in 350° F (180° C) oven for 15 to 20 minutes. Or grill tortillas over medium heat for 30 to 60 seconds per side.

◆

Instead of turkey, use 4 boneless, skinless chicken breasts; using a sharp knife, cut each chicken breast horizontally along one long side to make 2 thin pieces.

1 lb	boneless turkey breast, cut into 1/4-inch (5 mm) slices	5(
1 tbsp	fresh lime juice	15 mL
1	clove garlic, minced	1
1/2 tsp	dried oregano	2 mL
1/2 tsp	ground cumin	2 mL
1/2 tsp	ground coriander	2 mL
1/2 tsp	salt	2 mL
Pinch	cayenne pepper	Pinch
2 tbsp	olive oil	25 mL
1	medium red onion, thinly sliced	1
1	small sweet red pepper, cut into thin 2-inch (5 cm) strips	1
1	small sweet green pepper, cut into thin 2-inch (5 cm) strips	1
8	flour tortillas (8-inch [20 cm] size), warmed	8
	Garnishes: Salsa, sour cream, shredded lettuce and shredded cheddar cheese	

1. In a bowl toss turkey with lime juice, garlic, oregano, cumin, coriander, salt and cayenne pepper. Marinate for 15 minutes at room temperature, or longer in the refrigerator.

2. In a large nonstick skillet, heat half the oil over high heat; cook turkey for 2 to 3 minutes per side, or until lightly browned and no longer pink in center. Transfer to plate; keep warm.

3. Add remaining oil to skillet; cook onion and peppers, stirring, for 3 minutes or until tender-crisp. Remove from heat. Cut turkey into thin diagonal strips; toss with onion-pepper mixture. Spoon turkey mixture down center of each tortilla; add a small spoonful of salsa and sour cream, if desired, and sprinkle with shredded lettuce and cheese. Roll up.

sole and haddock. As much as I like to quickly fry a crumb-coated fillet in a skillet on the stovetop, only 1 or 2 can fit comfortably in the pan at one time. Hence the speed and practicality of cooking all the fillets at once by the oven method. Increase time accordingly for thicker fillets.

TIP

If using individually frozen fish fillets, place on a microwave-safe rack or large plate in single layer. Microwave at Medium for 3 to 5 minutes, rearranging twice, or until just a few ice crystals remain. Let stand for 10 minutes to defrost completely.

Crispy Almond Baked Fish

Preheat oven to 425° F (220° C)
Baking sheet

1/2 cup	soft bread crumbs	125 mL
1/3 cup	sliced blanched almonds	75 mL
1/2 tsp	dried tarragon *or* basil	2 mL
1/2 tsp	grated orange *or* lemon rind	2 mL
1 lb	fish fillets, such as sole, haddock or turbot	500 g
2 tbsp	melted butter	25 mL
	Salt and pepper	
	Lemon wedges	

1. In a food processor combine bread crumbs, almonds, tarragon and orange rind. Process, using on-off turns, until almonds are finely chopped.

2. Wrap fish in paper towels to absorb excess moisture. Brush baking sheet with some of the melted butter. Arrange fillets on sheet in single layer. Brush tops with remaining butter; season with salt and pepper. Sprinkle crumbs over fish and pat lightly.

3. Bake in preheated oven for 8 to 10 minutes or until fish flakes when tested with a fork. (Time depends on thickness of fish; increase time accordingly). Serve with lemon wedges.

AMAZING CHILI (PAGE 55) ➤

OVERLEAF: CAESAR SALAD (PAGE 130) ➤

Easy Lasagna

Serves 8

Everyone loves lasagna but who has the time to make it from scratch?

Try this streamlined version that makes even a non-cook look like a pro in the kitchen. It's also the perfect recipe for young cooks, since there's no chopping involved. Once you assemble the ingredients, it takes a mere 15 minutes to prepare and the lasagna is ready for the oven.

TIP

Lasagna freezes well; cover with plastic wrap then with foil and freeze. Let defrost in the refrigerator overnight before baking.

Preheat oven to 350° F (180° C)
13- by 9-inch (3 L) baking dish, lightly greased

2 cups	ricotta cheese	500 mL
1/3 cup	freshly grated Parmesan cheese	75 mL
2	large eggs, beaten	2
1/4 tsp	pepper	1 mL
1/4 tsp	nutmeg	1 mL
12	precooked lasagna noodles	12
3 cups	spaghetti sauce (homemade or store-bought)	750 mL
2 cups	shredded mozzarella cheese	500 mL

1. In a bowl combine ricotta, eggs and Parmesan cheese; season with pepper and nutmeg.

2. Depending on thickness of the spaghetti sauce, add about 3/4 cup (175 mL) water to thin sauce. (Precooked noodles absorb extra moisture while cooking.)

3. Spoon 1/2 cup (125 mL) sauce in bottom of prepared baking dish. Layer with 3 lasagna noodles. Spread with 3/4 cup (175 mL) of the sauce and then one-third of the ricotta mixture. Repeat with 2 more layers of noodles, sauce and ricotta cheese. Layer with rest of noodles and top with remaining sauce. Sprinkle with mozzarella cheese.

4. Bake, uncovered, in preheated oven for 45 minutes or until cheese is melted and sauce is bubbly.

≺ BROCCOLI AND CHEESE-STUFFED POTATOES (PAGE 85)

PASTA AND GRAINS

Tuna Noodle Bake with Cheddar Crumb Topping

Serves 4 to 6

This recipe takes an old standby to new heights. What's great, too, is that it keeps well in the fridge for up to 2 days before baking. Just pop it in the oven when you get home from work for an effortless meal. Serve with a crisp green salad.

TIP

To make ahead, cook noodles, rinse under cold water to chill; drain. Combine cold noodles and cold sauce; spoon into casserole dish, cover and refrigerate. Add crumb topping just before baking to prevent it from getting soggy.

Preheat oven to 350° F (180° C)
13- by 9-inch (3 L) casserole dish, lightly greased

1 tbsp	butter	15 mL
8 oz	mushrooms, sliced	250 g
3/4 cup	chopped green onions	175 mL
2 tbsp	all-purpose flour	25 mL
1	can (10 oz [284 mL]) chicken broth, undiluted	1
1 cup	milk	250 mL
4 oz	light cream cheese, softened and cubed	125 g
1	can (6 1/2 oz [184 g]) solid white tuna, drained and flaked	1
1 cup	frozen peas	250 mL
8 oz	broad egg noodles	250 g

Crumb Topping:

1/2 cup	dry bread crumbs	125 mL
2 tbsp	melted butter	25 mL
1 cup	shredded Cheddar cheese	250 mL

1. In a saucepan melt butter over medium heat. Add mushrooms and green onions; cook, stirring, for 3 minutes or until softened.

2. Blend in flour; pour in broth and milk. Bring to a boil, stirring constantly, until slightly thickened. Stir in cream cheese until melted. Add tuna and peas; cook 2 minutes more or util heated through. Remove from heat.

3. Cook noodles in a large pot of boiling water until tender but still firm. Drain well. Stir noodles into sauce. Spoon into prepared casserole dish.

4. Make the crumb topping: In a bowl toss bread crumbs with melted butter; add Cheddar cheese. Just before baking, sprinkle topping over noodles.

5. Bake in preheated oven for about 30 minutes (10 minutes longer if refrigerated) or until top is golden.

Best-Ever Macaroni and Cheese

Serves 4 to 6

As popular today as in the 1950s, classic macaroni and cheese has a lot going for it. It's not hard to make, so why open up a box of the pre-packaged stuff when you can create the real thing in your kitchen?

TIP

You can ruin a good pasta dish if you don't cook the pasta properly. The most common error is not using enough water to boil the pasta — with the result that it cooks unevenly and sticks together.

How to cook 1 lb (500 g) of pasta: Using a large pot, bring 16 cups (4 L) of water to a full rolling boil. Add 1 tbsp (15 mL) salt (this is important for flavor) and all the pasta at once. (Do not add oil.) Stir immediately to prevent pasta from sticking. Cover with a lid to return water quickly to full boil. Then uncover and stir occasionally. Taste to see if pasta is *al dente*, or firm to the bite. Drain immediately. Unless directed otherwise, ever rinse pasta — this chills it and removes the coating of starch that helps sauce cling to pasta. Return to pot or place in large warmed serving bowl; add the sauce and toss until well-coated. (Never plunk pasta on serving plates and ladle sauce on top.) Serve immediately.

Preheat oven to 375° F (190° C)
8-cup (2 L) deep casserole dish, buttered

Cheese Sauce:

3 tbsp	butter	45 mL
1/4 cup	all-purpose flour	50 mL
1	bay leaf	1
3 cups	milk	750 mL
1 tbsp	Dijon mustard	15 mL
	Salt and cayenne pepper	
2 cups	shredded Cheddar cheese (about 8 oz [250 g]), preferably aged	500 mL
2 cups	elbow macaroni	500 mL
1 tbsp	butter	15 mL
1 cup	soft bread crumbs	250 mL

1. In a large saucepan, melt butter over medium heat. Blend in flour and add bay leaf; cook, stirring, for 30 seconds. Pour in 1 cup (250 mL) of the milk, whisking constantly, until mixture comes to a boil and is very thick. Pour in rest of milk in a slow stream, whisking constantly, until sauce comes to a full boil and is smooth. Whisk in mustard.

2. Reduce heat to low; stir in cheese until melted. Remove bay leaf; season with salt and a dash of cayenne pepper to taste. Remove from heat.

3. Meanwhile, in a large pot of boiling salted water, cook macaroni for 8 minutes or until just tender. (Do not overcook; pasta continues to cook in sauce.) Drain well. Stir into cheese sauce until well coated.

4. Spoon into prepared casserole dish. In a bowl microwave remaining 1 tbsp (15 mL) butter at High for 20 seconds or until melted. Toss with bread crumbs; sprinkle over top. Bake in preheated oven for 25 minutes or until bubbly and top is lightly browned.

Big-Batch Tomato Sauce

Makes about 7 cups (1.75 L)

Here's an indispensable sauce I always have handy in the freezer to use as a base for my family's favorite pasta dishes. It's a versatile sauce and I've included several ways to serve it.

TIP

In summer, instead of canned tomatoes, I make this sauce with 5 lbs (2.5 kg) of fresh ripe tomatoes, preferably the plum variety To prepare, remove tomato cores; cut an X in the bottom of each. Plunge in boiling water for 30 seconds to loosen skins. Chill in cold water; drain. Slip off skins; cut tomatoes in half cross-wise and squeeze out seeds. Chop finely.

◆

Instead of dried basil and oregano, replace dried herbs with 1/3 cup (75 mL) chopped fresh basil; add towards end of cooking.

◆

To save time, chop vegetables in the food processor.

◆

For a smooth sauce, I like to purée the canned tomatoes in the food processor before adding.

2 tbsp	olive oil	25 mL
1	medium onion, finely chopped	1
2	medium carrots, peeled and finely chopped	2
1	stalk celery, including leaves, finely chopped	1
4	cloves garlic, finely chopped	4
1 tbsp	dried basil	15 mL
1 1/2 tsp	dried oregano	7 mL
1 tsp	salt	5 mL
1 tsp	granulated sugar	5 mL
1/2 tsp	pepper	2 mL
1	bay leaf	1
2	cans (28 oz [796 mL]) plum tomatoes, chopped	2
1	can (5 1/2 oz [156 mL]) tomato paste	1
1/4 cup	finely chopped fresh parsley	50 mL

1. In a Dutch oven, heat oil over medium-high heat. Add onion, carrots, celery, garlic, basil, oregano, salt, sugar, pepper and bay leaf; cook, stirring often, for 5 minutes or until vegetables are softened.

2. Stir in tomatoes, tomato paste and 1 tomato-paste can of water. Bring to a boil; reduce heat and simmer, partially covered, for 35 to 40 minutes, stirring occasionally, until slightly thickened. Remove bay leaf; stir in parsley. Let cool; pack into containers and refrigerate or freeze.

Spaghetti with Meatballs

Serves 4

1. In a large saucepan, combine 3 cups (750 mL) BIG-BATCH TOMATO SAUCE, half-recipe BASIC MEATBALLS (see recipe, page 27) and 1/2 cup (125 mL) beef stock. Bring to a boil, reduce heat and simmer, covered, for 15 minutes. Toss with 12 oz (375 g) cooked spaghetti or other string pasta; sprinkle with Parmesan cheese.

Spaghetti with Meat Sauce

Serves 4

1. In a large nonstick skillet over medium-high heat, cook 12 oz (375 g) lean ground beef (or use part ground veal or pork), crushing with back of spoon, for 5 minutes, or until no longer pink. Add 1/2 cup (125 mL) red wine or beef stock; cook until partly reduced.

2. Stir in 3 cups (750 mL) BIG-BATCH TOMATO SAUCE; season with salt, pepper and pinch of red pepper flakes, if desired. Reduce heat, cover and simmer for 15 minutes. Toss with 12 oz (375 g) cooked string pasta such as spaghetti or tube pasta such as penne or rigatoni. Sprinkle with Parmesan cheese.

Tortellini with Creamy Tomato Sauce

Serves 3

1 1/2 cups	BIG-BATCH TOMATO SAUCE (see recipe, page 102)	375 mL
1/2 cup	whipping (35%) cream	125 mL
8 oz	cheese- or meat-stuffed tortellini	250 g

1. In a large saucepan over medium heat, combine tomato sauce and whipping cream; bring to a boil. (Do not substitute light cream as it may curdle). Reduce heat to medium-low and simmer, partially covered, for 5 minutes or until slightly thickened.

2. Cook tortellini until just tender; drain and toss with sauce.

Fettuccine Alfredo

Serves 6

This luxurious pasta delivers so much pleasure it's worth the calorie splurge once in a while. Serve it on special occasions as a main course or as a starter dish. *Delicioso!*

The creamy flavor of fettuccine Alfredo comes not only from the cream and butter but also from the quality of the Parmesan cheese. You're in for a rich and nutty-sweet treat when you indulge in a morsel of *Parmigiano Reggiano* or its less-aged (and milder) cousin, *Grana Padano*. There's just no comparison between authentic Parmesan and the containers of inferior boxed grated cheese found on supermarket shelves.

◆

Like coffee, Parmesan looses its wonderful aromatic flavor and moisture if grated ahead. Choose a wedge in a cheese shop and have it grated for you. Or better still, grate the cheese as you need it. You can also serve it as a table cheese — another excellent way to appreciate this regal cheese.

◆

Store Parmesan wedges wrapped in plastic wrap, then in foil, in the refrigerator; it keeps well for weeks.

1 cup	whipping (35%) cream	250 mL
1 cup	light (15%) cream	250 mL
1/4 cup	butter, softened	50 mL
1 1/2 cups	freshly grated Parmesan cheese	375 mL
1/4 tsp	freshly ground pepper	1 mL
	Salt and nutmeg	
1 lb	fettuccine	500 g
1/4 cup	finely chopped fresh chives *or* basil *or* parsley	50 mL

1. In a large saucepan, bring whipping cream and light cream to a boil over medium heat; boil until reduced to about 1 1/2 cups (375 mL). Reduce heat to low; whisk in butter and cheese until sauce is smooth. Add pepper; season with salt and nutmeg to taste. Keep warm.

2. Meanwhile, in a large pot of boiling salted water, cook the pasta until tender but still firm. Drain well; return to pot; pour cream sauce over. Sprinkle with herbs; toss well. Serve immediately on warm plates.

Party Pasta with Mushrooms, Spinach and Tomato

Serves 8

Planning a party — or going to one?

This meatless dish is perfect to serve company or take along to a pot luck supper. It makes a large party dish or you can divide it into smaller portions and place into two 8-inch (2 L) casserole dishes. Enjoy one now and freeze the other for another delicious meal.

TIP

Here are some general guidelines for making pasta dishes ahead and refrigerating or freezing:

Make pasta sauces up to 2 days ahead and refrigerate or freeze for up to 2 months.

If assembling pasta dish ahead: Cook pasta and chill under cold water; drain. Toss cold pasta with cold sauce and spoon into casserole dish. It's best to assemble casserole no more than a few hours ahead to prevent pasta from absorbing too much of the sauce.

To freeze: Do not add the cheese topping (it goes rubbery when frozen). Cover with plastic wrap, then with foil. Freeze for up to 2 months. Let defrost in refrigerator overnight. Increase baking time by about 10 minutes.

Preheat oven to 350° F (180° C)
13- by 9-inch (3 L) baking dish, lightly greased

2 tbsp	butter	25 mL
1	medium onion, finely chopped	1
4	cloves garlic, minced	4
12 oz	sliced mushrooms	375 g
1 tsp	dried basil	5 mL
1 tsp	dried oregano	5 mL
1 tsp	dried marjoram	5 mL
1 tsp	salt	5 mL
1/2 tsp	crumbled dried rosemary	2 mL
1/2 tsp	pepper	2 mL
1/4 cup	all-purpose flour	50 mL
1 1/2 cups	milk	375 mL
2 cups	light (15%) cream	500 mL
1	can (28 oz [796 mL]) tomatoes, drained, juice reserved, chopped	1
2	pkgs (10 oz [300 g] each) fresh or frozen spinach, cooked, squeezed dry and chopped	2
1 lb	bow-tie pasta (farfalle)	500 g
2 cups	shredded Fontina *or* Provolone cheese	500 mL
1/2 cup	freshly grated Parmesan cheese	125 mL

1. In a large saucepan or Dutch oven, melt butter over medium-high heat. Add onion, garlic, mushrooms, basil, oregano, marjoram, salt, rosemary and pepper; cook, stirring often, for 5 minutes or until softened.

2. In a bowl blend flour with just enough milk to make a smooth paste; stir in remaining milk. Gradually add milk mixture and cream to mushroom mixture, stirring constantly, until sauce comes to a full boil and thickens.

3. Add tomatoes with juice and spinach; cook, stirring often, for 3 to 5 minutes, or until piping hot. Adjust seasoning with salt and pepper to taste. Let sauce cool to room temperature.

4. Meanwhile, cook pasta in a large pot of boiling salted water until tender but firm. Drain well. Return pasta to pot and stir in sauce until coated.

5. Place half the pasta in prepared baking dish. Sprinkle with half the Fontina and half the Parmesan cheese. Layer with rest of pasta and sprinkle with remaining Fontina and Parmesan cheese.

6. Bake, uncovered, in preheated oven for 35 to 40 minutes or until center is piping hot and top is lightly browned. Serve immediately.

Turkey Chili with Pasta and Vegetables

Serves 4

Kids love this dish and so do grown-ups. The spicy Mexican influence provides a nice change from the traditional Italian pasta fare.

Adjust this one-dish meal according to your family's tastes — possibly by substituting favorite vegetables, such as corn and green peppers, for the zucchini. Omit red pepper flakes if you prefer a milder-tasting dish.

◆

For an Italian version, substitute 1 1/2 tsp (7 mL) dried basil for the chili powder and cumin.

Try this vegetarian version:

Chickpea Chili with Pasta and Vegetables
Omit ground turkey. Cook vegetables and seasonings in 1 tbsp (15 mL) vegetable oil. Add 1 can (19 oz [540 mL]) chickpeas, drained and rinsed, along with canned tomatoes.

1 lb	lean ground turkey *or* ground chicken	500 g
1	medium onion, chopped	1
2	cloves garlic, finely chopped	2
2	carrots, peeled and diced	2
2	stalks celery, chopped	2
1 tbsp	chili powder	15 mL
1 tsp	dried oregano	5 mL
1 tsp	ground cumin	5 mL
1/2 tsp	salt	2 mL
1/4 tsp	red pepper flakes, or to taste	1 mL
1	can (28 oz [796 mL]) plum tomatoes, juice reserved, chopped	1
2	small zucchini, halved lengthwise and sliced	2
1 1/2 cups	elbow macaroni or other small shaped pasta such as shells	375 mL

1. In a Dutch oven, cook meat over medium-high heat, breaking up lumps with the back of a spoon, for 5 minutes or until no longer pink.

2. Add onion, garlic, carrots, celery, chili powder, oregano, cumin, salt and red pepper flakes; cook, stirring often, for 5 minutes or until vegetables are softened.

3. Stir in tomatoes with juice. Bring to a boil; reduce heat to medium-low. Cover and simmer, stirring occasionally, for 20 minutes.

4. Meanwhile, in a large pot of boiling salted water, cook pasta for 8 minutes or until just tender but still firm. Drain well; stir into tomato mixture along with zucchini; cook 5 to 7 minutes more or until zucchini is just tender. Adjust seasoning with salt and pepper to taste.

Spicy Noodles with Vegetables and Peanut Sauce

Serves 6

My vegetarian daughter requests this dish whenever she invites her teenage friends to the house for dinner. It's her idea of a comfort food — a vibrant combination of Asian flavors that tastes terrific and is nourishing, too. Any leftovers make a great next-day lunch.

TIP

Cut vegetables into uniform 2-inch (5 cm) lengths. This colorful pasta dish takes only a few minutes to cook, so have ingredients assembled before you start.

Peanut Sauce:

1/4 cup	peanut butter	50 mL
1/3 cup	water	75 mL
2 tbsp	soya sauce	25 mL
2 tbsp	lime juice	25 mL
2 tbsp	brown sugar	25 mL
1/4 tsp	red pepper flakes, or to taste	1 mL
1 tbsp	sesame oil	15 mL
2 tbsp	vegetable oil	25 mL
1 tbsp	minced ginger root	15 mL
2	cloves garlic, minced	2
1	leek, white and light green part only, cut into matchstick strips	1
2	small Italian eggplants, cut into thin strips (about 2 cups [500 mL])	2
2	sweet peppers (assorted colors), seeded and cut into thin strips	2
12 oz	linguine, broken into thirds	375 g
1/2 cup	chopped fresh coriander *or* parsley	125 mL

1. Make the peanut sauce: In a small saucepan, combine peanut butter, water, soya sauce, lime juice, brown sugar, red pepper flakes and sesame oil. Stir over medium heat until mixture is warm and smooth. (Or microwave at High for 2 minutes, stirring twice.) Set aside.

2. In wok or large nonstick skillet, heat oil over high heat. Add ginger root, garlic, leek and eggplant; cook, stirring, for 2 minutes. Add peppers; cook, stirring, for 1 minute more or until vegetables are just tender-crisp. Stir in peanut sauce until heated through.

3. Meanwhile, in a large pot of boiling salted water, cook linguine until tender but firm. Drain and return to pot. Toss with vegetables and peanut sauce until well coated; sprinkle with coriander. Serve warm or at room temperature.

Rigatoni with Roasted Ratatouille Sauce

Serves 4 to 6

Chockfull of vegetables, this zesty tomato sauce can be used in a variety of ways. I use it as a pizza sauce, as a topping for creamy polenta, or to dress baked potatoes. Instead of sautéeing the vegetables in batches on the stovetop, I've streamlined the method by roasting them in the oven.

TIP

Red pepper flakes are sold with a variety of names, including crushed dried chilies or hot chili pepper flakes. You can find them in supermarkets and in bulk foods shops. Other sources of hot seasonings such as cayenne pepper can be substituted, but use slightly less (it's hotter).

Preheat oven to 400° F (200° C)
12- by 8-inch (2.5 L) shallow baking dish

1	eggplant (about 1 lb [500 g])	1
2	medium zucchini (about 12 oz [375 g])	2
1	large sweet red pepper	1
2 tbsp	olive oil	25 mL
	Salt and pepper	
1	large onion, finely chopped	1
2	large cloves garlic, minced	2
1 tsp	dried basil	5 mL
1 tsp	dried oregano	5 mL
1/4 tsp	dried thyme	1 mL
1/4 tsp	red pepper flakes, or to taste	1 mL
1	can (28 oz [796 mL]) plum tomatoes, juice reserved, chopped	1
1/4 cup	chopped fresh parsley	50 mL
8 oz	rigatoni or other tube-shaped pasta	250 g
1 1/2 cups	shredded mozzarella *or* Provolone cheese	375 mL

1. Cut eggplant, zucchini and peppers into 3/4-inch (2 cm) cubes. Arrange vegetables on oiled rimmed baking sheet. Toss with 1 tbsp (15 mL) of the oil; season with salt and pepper.

2. Roast, uncovered, in preheated oven, stirring occasionally, for 35 minutes or until vegetables are tender and lightly colored.

3. Meanwhile, in a large saucepan, heat remaining oil over medium heat. Add onion, garlic, basil, oregano, salt, sugar, thyme and red pepper flakes; cook, stirring often, for 4 minutes or until softened.

4. Add tomatoes with juice; bring to a boil, reduce heat to medium-low and simmer, partially covered, for 20 minutes.

5. Add roasted vegetables and parsley; simmer for 5 minutes to blend flavors. Adjust seasoning with salt and pepper to taste.

6. Cook pasta in a large pot of boiling salted water until tender but firm. Drain well. Toss with vegetable sauce; spoon into baking dish. Sprinkle with cheese.

7. Bake in preheated oven for 25 to 30 minutes (10 minutes longer if refrigerated) or until bubbly and cheese is lightly colored.

Baked Penne with Italian Sausage and Sweet Peppers

Serves 6

This hearty pasta dish, brimming with chunks of tasty sausage and colorful peppers, makes a delicious feast for any occasion.

TIP

Add 1/3 cup (75 mL) small black olives to the sauce along with the parsley for an added dimension of flavor. For a vegetarian version, omit the sausages.

Preheat oven to 350° F (180° C)
13- by 9-inch (3 L) baking dish, lightly oiled

2 tbsp	olive oil	25 mL
12 oz	hot or mild Italian sausages	375 g
3	sweet peppers (assorted colors)	3
1	large onion, halved lengthwise and thinly sliced	1
2	garlic cloves, finely chopped	2
1 tsp	dried basil	5 mL
1 tsp	dried oregano	5 mL
1/2 tsp	salt	2 mL
1/2 tsp	red pepper flakes, or to taste	2 mL
1	can (28 oz [796 mL]) plum tomatoes, juice reserved, chopped	1
1/4 cup	chopped sun-dried tomatoes (optional)	50 mL
1/4 cup	chopped fresh parsley	50 mL
12 oz	penne or other small tube-shaped pasta	375 g
1 1/2 cups	grated Fontina *or* mozzarella cheese	375 mL
1/3 cup	freshly grated Romano *or* Parmesan cheese	75 mL

1. Prick skins of sausages with a fork. In a Dutch oven or large saucepan, heat 1 tbsp (15 mL) of the oil over medium-high heat; cook sausages for 5 minutes or until browned on all sides. (Sausages will not be cooked through.) Remove from pan, cut into slices and reserve.

2. Add remaining oil to pan. Add peppers, onion, garlic, basil, oregano, salt and red pepper flakes; cook, stirring often, for 7 minutes or until softened.

3. Return sausage slices to pan along with canned tomatoes with juice and sun-dried tomatoes, if using. Bring to a boil; reduce heat to medium-low; cover and simmer, stirring occasionally, for 20 minutes. Stir in parsley. Adjust seasoning with salt, if necessary.

4. Meanwhile, cook pasta in a large pot of boiling salted water until tender but firm. Drain well. Place half of the cooked pasta in prepared baking dish. Pour half of the sauce over. Layer again with remaining pasta and top with remaining sauce.

5. In a bowl combine Fontina and Romano cheeses; sprinkle over top of casserole. Bake, uncovered, in preheated oven for 30 to 35 minutes or until cheese is melted and lightly colored.

Molasses Baked Beans

Serves 8

Here's an old-time favorite that stirs memories of the pioneer spirit. This rustic dish is a winter standby and wonderful when served with home-baked bread.

For a vegetarian version, omit bacon and cook onions and garlic in 2 tbsp (25 mL) vegetable oil.

Preheat oven to 300° F (150° C)
12-cup (3 L) casserole dish or bean pot

1 lb	dried Great Northern or white pea beans (about 2 1/4 cups [550 mL]), rinsed and picked over	500 g
6	slices lean smoky bacon, chopped	6
1	large onion, chopped	1
3	cloves garlic, finely chopped	3
1	can (7 1/2 oz [213 mL]) tomato sauce	1
1/3 cup	molasses	75 mL
1/4 cup	packed brown sugar	50 mL
2 tbsp	balsamic vinegar	25 mL
2 tsp	dry mustard	10 mL
1 tsp	salt	5 mL
1/4 tsp	pepper	1 mL

1. In a Dutch oven, combine beans with 6 cups (1.5 L) cold water. Bring to a boil over high heat; boil for 2 minutes. Remove from heat, cover and let stand for 1 hour.

2. Drain beans and cover with 8 cups (2 L) cold water. Bring to a boil; reduce heat, cover and simmer for 30 to 40 minutes or until beans are just tender but still hold their shape. Drain, reserving 2 cups (500 mL) cooking liquid. Place beans in casserole dish or bean pot.

3. Meanwhile, in a saucepan, cook bacon over medium heat, stirring often, for 5 minutes or until crisp. Drain all but 2 tbsp (25 mL) fat in pan. Add onions and garlic; cook, stirring, for 3 minutes or until softened.

4. Add 2 cups (500 mL) reserved bean-cooking liquid, tomato sauce, molasses, brown sugar, balsamic vinegar, mustard, salt and pepper. Stir into beans.

5. Cover and bake in preheated oven for 2 1/2 to 3 hours or until most of liquid has been absorbed.

Herbed Rice Pilaf

Serves 6 to 8

This herb-infused rice makes
the perfect accompaniment
to a wide range of dishes.
Try it with fish, chicken,
beef, lamb or pork.

TIP

To save time, make ahead
and reheat in the microwave
before serving.

VARIATION

Saffron Rice Pilaf
Substitute 1/4 tsp (1 mL)
crushed saffron threads for
the thyme.

2 tbsp	butter	25 mL
1	small onion, finely chopped	1
1	clove garlic, minced	1
1/2 tsp	dried thyme	2 mL
	Pepper to taste	
1 1/2 cups	long grain rice	375 mL
3 cups	chicken stock *or* vegetable stock	750 mL
1	small sweet red pepper, finely diced	1
1/4 cup	chopped fresh parsley	50 mL

1. In a large saucepan, melt butter over medium heat.
   Add onion, garlic, thyme and pepper; cook, stirring
   often, for 3 minutes or until softened.

2. Add rice and stock; bring to a boil. Reduce heat to low;
   cover and simmer for 15 minutes or until most of stock
   is absorbed.

3. Stir in red pepper; cover and cook for 7 to 9 minutes
   more or until rice is tender. Stir in parsley; let stand,
   uncovered, for 5 minutes.

Wild Mushroom Risotto

Serves 4 to 6

Risotto is hugely popular these days. And no wonder — its creamy appeal makes it a modern comfort food. It may seem intimidating to make at home, but it's easy to do provided you don't wander away from the stove. What else is key about risotto? It waits for no one, so call everyone to the table as you add the last ladle of stock to the saucepan.

TIP

A proper risotto is made with Italian short grain rice, which has a relatively high starch content. As it cooks, it gives off the starch and the constant stirring results in a creamy, moist texture similar to porridge.

◆

Arborio rice is the most widely available short grain variety; look for the word *superfino* on the package to ensure you are buying a superior grade. *Vialone nano* and *carnaroli* are two other types of short grain Italian rice that make wonderful risotto. They are not quite as starchy as Arborio and require slightly less stock in cooking.

5 cups	lightly salted chicken stock *or* vegetable stock (approximate)	1.25 L
2 tbsp	butter	25 mL
2 tbsp	olive oil	25 mL
1 lb	assorted wild mushrooms, such as cremini, shiitake and oyster, coarsely chopped	500 g
2	cloves garlic, minced	2
1 tbsp	chopped fresh thyme (*or* 1 tsp [5 mL] dried)	15 mL
1/4 tsp	pepper	1 mL
1	small onion, finely chopped	1
1 1/2 cups	short grain Italian rice (Arborio)	375 mL
1/2 cup	white wine *or* stock	125 mL
1/3 cup	freshly grated Parmesan cheese	75 mL
	Salt	
2 tbsp	chopped fresh parsley	25 mL

1. In a large saucepan, bring stock to a boil; reduce heat to low and keep hot.

2. In a heavy-bottomed medium saucepan, heat 1 tbsp (15 mL) each oil and butter over medium heat. Add mushrooms, garlic, thyme and pepper; cook, stirring often, for 5 to 7 minutes or until tender. Remove and set aside.

3. Add remaining butter and oil to saucepan; cook onion, stirring, for 2 minutes or until softened. Add rice; stir for 1 minute. Add wine; stir until absorbed.

4. Add 1 cup (250 mL) of the hot stock; adjust heat to a simmer so stock bubbles and is absorbed slowly.

5. When absorbed, continue adding 1 cup (250 mL) stock at a time, stirring almost constantly, for 15 minutes. Add mushroom mixture; cook, stirring often, adding more stock when absorbed, until rice is just tender but slightly firm in the center. Mixture should be creamy; add more stock or water, if necessary. (Total cooking time will be 20 to 25 minutes.)

6. Add Parmesan cheese; adjust seasoning with salt and pepper to taste. Spoon into warm shallow serving bowls or onto plates. Sprinkle with parsley; serve immediately.

VEGETABLES AND SALADS

Gruyere Scalloped Potatoes

Serves 4 to 6

Some people think there can never be enough potato recipes in a cookbook — and I agree. Potatoes are soothing, earthy and one of the best comfort foods around. No matter how you prepare them they always taste wonderful.

Here's an update of a French classic with half the calorie-rich cream replaced by flavorful stock. It's a perfect accompaniment to a Sunday roast or as a main course dish served with a crisp tossed salad.

TIP

Recipe can easily be doubled and baked in a 13- by 9-inch (3 L) baking dish.

Preheat oven to 375° F (190° C)
9-inch (2.5 L) round or square baking dish, buttered

2 lbs	russet or Yukon gold potatoes (about 6)	1 kg
	Salt, pepper and nutmeg	
1/2 cup	vegetable stock *or* chicken stock	125 mL
1/2 cup	whipping (35%) cream	125 mL
1	clove garlic, minced	1
1 cup	shredded Gruyere *or* Cheddar cheese	250 mL

1. Peel potatoes; cut into very thin slices using paring knife or slicing attachment on food processor. Arrange slices in prepared baking dish. Season with salt, pepper and nutmeg.

2. In a small saucepan, bring stock, cream and garlic to a boil. (Or place in a large glass measure; microwave at High for 2 1/2 minutes or until almost boiling.) Pour over potatoes. Cover with lid or foil.

3. Bake in preheated oven for 40 minutes. Sprinkle with cheese; bake, uncovered, for 20 to 25 minutes more or until cheese is bubbly and golden.

Asparagus with Parmesan and Toasted Almonds

Serves 6

When locally grown asparagus appears at the market, it's one of my rites of spring. I prepare them tossed with crunchy almonds and melting Parmesan — and it's every bit as pleasing as a buttery Hollandaise.

TIP

Try making this dish with green beans. Trim and cut into 1 1/2-inch (4 cm) lengths and cook in boiling water for about 5 minutes or until tender-crisp.

1 1/2 lbs	asparagus	750 g
1/4 cup	sliced blanched almonds	50 mL
2 tbsp	butter	25 mL
2	cloves garlic, finely chopped	2
1/4 cup	freshly grated Parmesan cheese	50 mL
	Salt and pepper	

1. Snap off asparagus ends; cut spears on the diagonal into 2-inch (5 cm) lengths. In a large nonstick skillet, bring 1/2 cup (125 mL) water to a boil; cook asparagus for 2 minutes (start timing when water returns to a boil) or until just tender-crisp. Run under cold water to chill; drain and reserve.

2. Dry the skillet; heat over medium heat. Add almonds and toast, stirring often, for 2 to 3 minutes or until golden. Remove and reserve.

3. Increase heat to medium-high. Add butter to skillet; cook asparagus and garlic, stirring, for 4 minutes or until asparagus is just tender.

4. Sprinkle with Parmesan; season with salt and pepper. Transfer to serving bowl; top with almonds.

Oven-Roasted Root Vegetables

Serves 6

I love the way oven-roasting sweetens and concentrates the flavors of these sturdy root vegetables. This dish is a natural with stew and mashed potatoes.

We're used to roasting potatoes, so moving onto other vegetables isn't that much of a shift in our cooking style. Try this treatment with other vegetables such as peppers, winter squash, beets, cauliflower and even asparagus. You'll be amazed with the results.
Use oil instead of butter and add a sprinkling of dried herbs, if you like. Reduce cooking time according to the size and type of vegetables.

Preheat oven to 400° F (200° C)
13- by 9-inch (3 L) baking dish, lightly oiled

3	medium carrots	3
2	medium parsnips	2
Half	small rutabaga (about 8 oz [250 g])	Half
1	medium red onion, cut into wedges	1
2	cloves garlic, cut into slivers	2
1/4 cup	dry sherry *or* chicken stock	50 mL
2 tbsp	melted butter	25 mL
1/2 tsp	salt	2 mL
1/4 tsp	pepper	1 mL
2 tbsp	finely chopped fresh parsley	25 mL

1. Peel carrots, parsnips and rutabaga; cut into 2- by 1/2-inch (5 by 1 cm) strips. Place in prepared baking dish along with onion and garlic.

2. In a small bowl, combine sherry and butter; drizzle over vegetables. Sprinkle with salt and pepper.

3. Cover dish with foil; bake 30 minutes. Remove foil; bake 25 to 30 minutes more, stirring occasionally, until vegetables are tender and light golden. Sprinkle with parsley before serving.

Cauliflower with Hazelnut Crumb Topping

Serves 6

Snowy cauliflower topped with cheese and nuts makes the perfect side dish for a Sunday roast. For vegetarians, it becomes a main course dish when served along with grains or a bowl of pasta.

TIP

Sprinkle the garlic-crumb mixture over other vegetables such as broccoli, Brussels sprouts or spinach. Unblanched almonds, pecans or walnuts can replace the hazelnuts.

Preheat broiler
12- by 8-inch (2.5 L) shallow baking dish

2 tbsp	butter	25 mL
1/4 cup	hazelnuts, finely chopped	50 mL
1/2 cup	soft bread crumbs	125 mL
1	large clove garlic, minced	1
1/2 cup	finely shredded Gruyere *or* aged Cheddar cheese	125 mL
2 tbsp	chopped fresh parsley	25 mL
1	medium head cauliflower, separated into florets	1

1. In a medium skillet, melt butter over medium heat. Add hazelnuts and cook, stirring, for 1 minute or until lightly toasted. Add bread crumbs and garlic; cook, stirring, for 1 minute more or until crumbs are lightly colored. Remove from heat; let cool.

2. In a bowl combine crumb mixture, cheese and parsley.

3. In a large saucepan of boiling salted water, cook cauliflower for 5 minutes or until tender-crisp. Drain well. Place in baking dish; sprinkle with crumb mixture. Place under preheated broiler for 1 to 2 minutes or until topping is lightly browned.

Orange Broccoli with Red Pepper

Serves 4

Broccoli is now so common on dinner plates, it has become the peas-and-carrots of the 1990s. And why not? Broccoli contains a wide range of beneficial nutrients such as Vitamin C and calcium. I usually steam broccoli, but I find that this quick stir-fry — with the lively taste of orange — makes for an interesting variation.

TIP

While North American tastes are generally restricted to broccoli florets, Asian cooking also uses broccoli stalks extensively. So don't throw them away — trim the woody bottoms and peel the stalks using a paring knife; then cut the tender, mild interior into slices or strips.

1/3 cup	orange juice	75 mL
1/2 tsp	cornstarch	2 mL
1 tbsp	olive oil	15 mL
4 cups	small broccoli florets and stalks, cut into 1 1/2- by 1/2-inch (4 by 1 cm) lengths	1 L
1	sweet red pepper, cut into 2- by 1/2-inch (5 by 1 cm) strips	1
1	clove garlic, minced	1
1 tsp	grated orange rind	5 mL
1/4 tsp	salt	1 mL
1/4 tsp	pepper	1 mL

1. In a glass measuring cup, stir together orange juice and cornstarch until smooth; reserve.

2. Heat oil in a large nonstick skillet over high heat. Add broccoli, red pepper and garlic; cook, stirring, for 2 minutes.

3. Add orange juice mixture; cover and cook 1 to 2 minutes or until vegetables are tender-crisp. Sprinkle with orange rind; season with salt and pepper. Serve immediately.

Green Beans Stewed with Tomatoes

Serves 4

This is a favorite dish to make in late summer when young beans and ripe tomatoes are at their best. But even in winter, with vine-ripened greenhouse tomatoes and imported fresh beans, this recipe is still good. If bits of tomato skin in the sauce bother you, peel the tomatoes before dicing.

TIP

For a quick supper, toss vegetable sauce with 8 oz (250 g) cooked pasta (such as penne) and sprinkle generously with Parmesan cheese. Also substitute other vegetables — such as fennel, asparagus or broccoli — for the beans.

1 lb	green beans	500 g
1 tbsp	olive oil	15 mL
1	small red onion, halved lengthwise, thinly sliced	1
2	cloves garlic, thinly sliced	2
1 tsp	dried basil	5 mL
2	ripe tomatoes, diced	2
1 tbsp	balsamic vinegar	15 mL
2 tbsp	water (approximate)	25 mL
1/4 tsp	salt	1 mL
1/4 tsp	pepper	1 mL
	Water	

1. Trim ends of beans; cut into 1 1/2-inch (4 cm) lengths. In a saucepan, cook beans in lightly salted boiling water, for 3 to 4 minutes (start timing when water returns to a boil) or until still crisp. Drain well; reserve.

2. Meanwhile, in a large nonstick skillet, heat oil over medium heat. Add onion, garlic and basil; cook, stirring, for 2 minutes or until softened.

3. Stir in tomatoes, vinegar, 2 tbsp (25 mL) water, salt and pepper; cook, stirring often, for 3 minutes or until sauce-like.

4. Add beans; cover and simmer for 8 to 10 minutes, stirring occasionally, until tender. Add more water, if necessary, to keep mixture moist. Serve warm or at room temperature.

Tomato, Zucchini and Potato Bake

**Serves 4 as main course
or 6 as side dish**

Don't even bother with meat. This melt-in-the-mouth veggie dish is a scrumptious meal in itself. Hearty potatoes, sweet tomatoes and delicate zucchini are heavenly when sprinkled with a golden cheese and crumb topping.

TIP

Just add warm crusty bread to this vegetable medley for an easy supper.

Preheat oven to 350° F (180° C)
13- by 9-inch (3 L) baking dish, lightly oiled

4	medium ripe tomatoes	4
	Salt	
2 tbsp	olive oil	25 mL
4	medium potatoes, peeled and thinly sliced	4
1	medium onion, thinly sliced	1
3	cloves garlic, finely chopped	3
1 1/2 tsp	dried Italian herbs *or* oregano	7 mL
	Pepper to taste	
3	small zucchini, thinly sliced (about 1 lb [500 g])	3
1 cup	shredded Gruyere *or* Provolone *or* mozzarella cheese	250 mL
1/4 cup	freshly grated Parmesan cheese	50 mL
1/2 cup	soft bread crumbs	125 mL
1/4 cup	finely chopped fresh parsley	50 mL

1. Halve tomatoes crosswise and squeeze out seeds. Thinly slice and place on paper towels to drain. Season lightly with salt.

2. In a large nonstick skillet, heat oil over medium heat. Add potatoes, onion, garlic and Italian herbs; cook, stirring often, for 8 to 10 minutes, or until potatoes are softened. Season with salt and pepper.

3. Layer half the sliced tomatoes, half the zucchini and half the potato mixture in prepared baking dish. Repeat layers again in same order. (The recipe can be prepared to this point up to 1 day ahead, then covered and refrigerated.)

4. In a bowl combine cheeses, bread crumbs and parsley; sprinkle over top.

5. Bake in preheated oven for 40 to 45 minutes or until top is golden and vegetables are tender.

Fluffy Garlic Mashed Potatoes

Serves 6

The secret to these creamy mashed potatoes is buttermilk. It adds a tangy flavor and keeps the potatoes moist so they reheat beautifully the next day.

The type of potatoes used determines how fluffy your mashed potatoes will be. The starchy russet or baking variety produces fluffy mashed potatoes. Yellow-fleshed potatoes such as Yukon Gold have a slightly buttery taste and make delicious mashed potatoes with a creamier texture. Regular white potatoes also make a creamy purée, although not as flavorful. New potatoes are not suitable for mashing as they don't have the starch content of storage potatoes.

◆

Adjust the amount of garlic you use depending on how much of a punch you want to give your potatoes.

To roast garlic: Trim 1/4 inch (5 mm) off the larger stem end of a whole bulb of garlic. Place cut-side down on a sheet of aluminum foil. Drizzle with 2 tsp (10 mL) olive oil. Wrap and place in small casserole dish. Roast in 350° F (180° C) oven for about 45 minutes or until soft. Squeeze the whole garlic bulb so pulp slips out of skins; add to potatoes when mashing. I often roast several heads at a time and refrigerate the roasted garlic to use during the week.

3 lbs	russet or Yukon Gold potatoes	1.5 kg
1/2 cup	milk	125 mL
2 tbsp	butter *or* olive oil	25 mL
2	cloves garlic (or more), finely chopped	2
3/4 to 1 cup	buttermilk *or* sour cream (approximate)	175 to 250 mL
	Salt and pepper or nutmeg	

1. Peel potatoes and cut into 3-inch (8 cm) chunks. In a large saucepan, cook potatoes in boiling salted water until tender, about 20 minutes or until fork-tender. (Yukon Gold potatoes take a few minutes longer.) Drain well and return to saucepan. Place over low heat and dry 1 to 2 minutes.

2. Put potatoes through a potato ricer or food mill, or mash with potato masher or use an electric mixer at low speed until very smooth. (Do not use a food processor or the potatoes will turn into glue.)

3. In a small saucepan, heat butter and garlic over medium-low heat for 1 to 2 minutes; do not let garlic brown. Add milk and heat until piping hot. Beat garlic mixture into potatoes along with enough buttermilk or sour cream to make a smooth purée. Adjust seasoning with salt and pepper or nutmeg to taste.

4. Place over medium heat, stirring occasionally, until potatoes are piping hot. Can be made a few hours ahead and reheated. Beat in additional milk or buttermilk to make potatoes creamy, if necessary.

VARIATION

Roasted Garlic Mashed Potatoes

Beat in a whole bulb of roasted garlic (instead of fresh garlic) in the above recipe. It may seem like a lot, but once roasted, garlic loses its harsh taste and becomes very mild and buttery.

Sweet-and-Sour Red Cabbage with Apples

Serves 8

I consider this recipe a convenience food. I keep containers of sweet-and-sour red cabbage in my freezer, ready to microwave at a moment's notice to serve along with pork chops or roasts.

TIP

Depending on how sweet-and-sour you like your red cabbage, add more brown sugar and vinegar to taste. Most cooked red cabbage recipes, this one included, call for vinegar or wine. This adds not only flavor, but acidity, which preserves the cabbage's bright red color.

◆

To freeze, pack cabbage into containers; it freezes well for up to 3 months.

2 tbsp	butter	25 mL
1	large onion, finely chopped	1
2	apples, peeled, cored and diced	2
1 cup	chicken stock *or* vegetable stock	250 mL
1/2 cup	red wine *or* additional stock	125 mL
1/3 cup	red wine vinegar	75 mL
1/3 cup	packed brown sugar	75 mL
1	bay leaf	1
1/2 tsp	salt	2 mL
1/4 tsp	cinnamon	1 mL
1/4 tsp	pepper	1 mL
Pinch	ground cloves	Pinch
1	medium red cabbage, finely shredded (about 10 cups [2.5 L])	1
1 1/2 tsp	cornstarch	7 mL
1 tbsp	cold water	15 mL

1. In a Dutch oven, heat butter over medium heat. Add onions and apples; cook, stirring often, for 5 minutes or until softened.

2. Add stock, wine, vinegar, brown sugar, bay leaf, salt, cinnamon, pepper and ground cloves. Bring to a boil; stir in cabbage.

3. Cover and simmer over medium-low heat, stirring occasionally, for 45 minutes or until cabbage is tender.

4. Blend cornstarch with water; stir into cabbage. Cook 3 minutes more or until sauce is slightly thickened. Remove bay leaf before serving.

BEST-EVER MACARONI AND CHEESE (PAGE 101) ➤

OVERLEAF: DOUBLE CHOCOLATE CHUNK COOKIES (PAGE 142) ➤

Lemon-Glazed Baby Carrots

Serves 4

This is one of my favorite choices to accompany a holiday roast or turkey. Packages of ready-to-cook, peeled whole baby carrots are widely available in supermarkets. They certainly make a cook's life easier — especially when you're preparing a mammoth family dinner and plan to serve several dishes.

TIP

If doubling the recipe, glaze vegetables in a large nonstick skillet to evaporate the stock quickly.

◆

Try this tasty treatment with a combination of blanched carrots, rutabaga and parsnip strips, too.

1 lb	peeled baby carrots	500 g
1/4 cup	chicken stock *or* vegetable stock	50 mL
1 tbsp	butter	15 mL
1 tbsp	brown sugar	15 mL
1 tbsp	lemon juice	15 mL
1/2 tsp	grated lemon rind	2 mL
1/4 tsp	salt	1 mL
	Pepper to taste	
1 tbsp	finely chopped fresh parsley *or* chives	15 mL

1. In a medium saucepan, cook carrots in boiling salted water for 5 to 7 minutes (start timing when water returns to a boil) or until just tender-crisp; drain and return to saucepan.

2. Add stock, butter, brown sugar, lemon juice and rind, salt and pepper. Cook, stirring often, 3 to 5 minutes or until liquid has evaporated and carrots are nicely glazed.

3. Sprinkle with parsley or chives and serve.

≺ SPAGHETTI WITH MEAT BALLS (PAGE 103)

Caesar Salad

Serves 6

The king of tossed salads was named after a Tijuana restaurateur by the name of Caesar Cardini. Here, mayonnaise gives this classic salad an even creamier texture than the original.

TIP

Raw or coddled eggs are considered taboo in salads because they may contain salmonella bacteria. Mayonnaise is used instead.

◆

Make sure salad greens are washed and dried thoroughly, preferably in a salad spinner, for best results. Homemade croutons make a definite flavor difference but 3 cups (750 mL) store-bought croutons work in a pinch.

◆

Anchovy fillets are best, but 1 tbsp (15 mL) anchovy paste can be used instead.

1/3 cup	olive oil	75 mL
2 tbsp	mayonnaise	25 mL
2 tbsp	fresh lemon juice	25 mL
2 tbsp	water	25 mL
1 tsp	Dijon mustard	5 mL
2	cloves garlic, finely chopped	2
3	anchovy fillets, chopped	3
1/4 tsp	pepper	1 mL
1	large head Romaine lettuce, torn into bite-sized pieces (about 12 cups [3 L])	1
6	slices bacon, cooked crisp and crumbled (optional)	6
	Garlic croutons (directions follow)	
1/3 cup	freshly grated Parmesan cheese	75 mL
	Salt	

1. In a food processor, combine oil, mayonnaise, lemon juice, water, mustard, garlic, anchovy fillets and pepper; process until smooth and creamy.

2. Arrange lettuce in salad bowl; pour dressing over and toss lightly. Add croutons; sprinkle with crumbled bacon, is using, and Parmesan cheese. Toss again. Taste and season with salt and pepper, if needed. Serve immediately.

GARLIC CROUTONS
Preheat oven to 375° F (190° C)

4 cups	cubed crusty bread, cut into 1/2-inch (1 cm) pieces	1 L
2 tbsp	olive oil	25 mL
1	clove garlic, minced	1
2 tbsp	freshly grated Parmesan cheese	25 mL

1. Place bread cubes in a bowl. Combine oil and garlic; drizzle over bread cubes and toss. Sprinkle with Parmesan and toss again. Arrange on baking sheet in single layer. Toast in preheated oven, stirring once, for about 10 minutes or until golden.

ALL ABOUT OLIVE OIL

- Olive oil is the pressed juice from olives, a fruit, and there are dozens of varieties, each with its own distinct flavor and characteristics.

- There are two grades of oil available in our market: **Extra virgin** is the best quality, retaining the fresh, natural flavor of the olives with a maximum acidity level of 1% oleic acid. It's ideal for cooking, salads and flavoring dishes before serving. **Regular** olive oil comes from olives that have been refined to produce a colorless and flavorless oil. Virgin oil is added to give it some added character. It is used primarily in cooking.

- What to look for in an oil: Olives oils are a lot like wines — there are many to choose from and they vary greatly in price and quality. Sample a variety to decide what appeals most to your taste buds, as well as budget.

- Read the bottle label to help you make an informed choice. Lower-priced brands of oils, although bottled in a particular country, are often a blend from several different countries in the Mediterranean. The more expensive olive oils, however, often include the name of the producer and region, along with a vintage date on their labels.

- Don't judge an oil by its color. Oils range from buttery yellow to vivid green depending on the olive variety and stage of ripeness at harvest time. Color does, however, give a clue to flavor. Generally, light-colored oils are more subtle than the robust darker oils.

- Olive oil loses it flavor and color over time, so use soon after purchase. Store oils in a cool, dark place, away from direct light. Do not store in the refrigerator. When properly capped, oil will keep for one year.

- "Light" olive oil is not lighter in calories, only in flavor. It's a refined oil and overpriced when compared to other quality oils in the same price bracket. If you want a mild-flavored oil, mix canola oil with some good-quality extra virgin instead.

- Olive oils add not only great flavor to foods, they have certain health advantages. Rich in monounsaturated fats, olive oils reduce the level of harmful cholesterol in our blood and at the same time leave the good cholesterol intact.

Layered Greek Salad

Serves 8 to 10

Remember the layered salads of the 1950s — the ones made with shredded iceberg lettuce, sliced cooked eggs and frozen peas crowned with heavy mayonnaise?
This updated version layers colorful vegetables that accent the flavors of Greece with a garlic-yogurt dressing and feta cheese topping.

TIP

To serve, spoon down through the vegetable layers so each serving has a little bit of everything.

4 cups	plain yogurt	1 L
2	cloves garlic, minced	2
2 tbsp	olive oil	25 mL
2 tbsp	red wine vinegar	25 mL
1 tsp	salt	5 mL
1 tsp	granulated sugar	5 mL
1 tsp	dried oregano	5 mL
1/4 tsp	pepper	1 mL
1	small head Romaine lettuce, shredded (about 8 cups [2 L], packed)	1
1	small Spanish onion, diced	1
1	sweet red pepper, diced	1
1	sweet green pepper, diced	1
Half	seedless cucumber, cubed	Half
1/4 cup	chopped fresh parsley	50 mL
1 cup	crumbled feta cheese	250 mL
2	ripe tomatoes, cut into wedges	2
12	Kalamata olives	12

1. Place yogurt in cheesecloth-lined sieve set over a bowl. Cover and refrigerate for 4 hours or until reduced to about 2 1/2 cups (625 mL). Transfer to bowl; discard whey. Stir in garlic, oil, vinegar, salt, sugar, oregano and pepper.

2. Line bottom of 8- or 9-inch (20 or 23 cm) round salad bowl with lettuce. Next, layer separately the onion, red pepper and cucumber.

3. Spread top with yogurt mixture. Refrigerate, loosely covered, for 8 hours or overnight. Sprinkle with parsley and feta. Garnish with tomatoes wedges and olives.

Couscous Salad with Basil and Pine Nuts

Serves 4

Ushered in on the new wave of Mediterranean cooking, couscous is a recent entrant in the world of comfort food. Like pasta — another comfort-food staple — couscous is made with semolina but, because it's precooked, needs only the addition of stock or water to reconstitute it. In minutes, you can whip up this delicious salad — great for a barbecue or pot luck supper.

TIP

Tender basil leaves bruise easily when chopped. Stack the leaves one on top of the other, roll up into a cigar shape and using a sharp knife, cut into fine thin shreds. To keep basil fresh like other fresh herbs (including parsley), wrap it in several layers of paper towel and place in a plastic bag; store in the warmest part of your fridge — in the butter keeper, for example, or the side door.

◆

If you can't find fresh basil, substitute 1/4 cup (50 mL) chopped fresh parsley and 1 tsp (5 mL) dried basil.

◆

Pine nuts are the buttery edible seeds of the pine tree. To toast, place in a dry skillet over medium heat, stirring constantly, until lightly toasted. Watch carefully — pine nuts are high in oil and burn easily.

1 cup	chicken stock *or* vegetable stock	250 mL
1 cup	couscous	250 mL
4	green onions, chopped	4
1	sweet red pepper, diced	1
1	medium zucchini, diced	1
1/4 cup	raisins	50 mL
1/4 cup	olive oil	50 mL
2 tbsp	red wine vinegar	25 mL
2 tbsp	orange juice	25 mL
1 tsp	grated orange rind	5 mL
1	large garlic clove, minced	1
1/2 tsp	salt	2 mL
	Pepper to taste	
1/4 cup	chopped fresh basil	50 mL
1/4 cup	toasted pine nuts	50 mL

1. Place couscous in a large bowl; pour stock over. Cover with a dinner plate and let stand for 5 minutes. Fluff with a fork to break up any lumps. Let cool to room temperature. Add onions, pepper, zucchini and raisins.

2. In a small bowl, whisk together oil, vinegar, orange juice and rind, garlic, salt and pepper. Pour over salad; toss well. Just before serving, stir in basil and pine nuts. Serve salad at room temperature.

To cook couscous as a side dish: Bring 1 1/4 cups (300 mL) stock or water to a boil along with 1 tbsp (15 mL) butter or oil. Add 1 cup (250 mL) couscous. Remove from heat; cover and let stand for 5 minutes. Fluff with fork; season with salt to taste.

Waldorf Coleslaw

Serves 6

A blend of two classics, this salad takes a traditional Waldorf — with celery, apples and walnuts — and mixes it with a good old-fashioned cabbage slaw. The combination is sublime.

VARIATION

Creamy Coleslaw
Substitute 2 peeled, shredded carrots for the celery; omit apples and walnuts.

8 cups	finely shredded green cabbage	2 L
5	green onions, chopped	5
2	large stalks celery, chopped	2
2	apples, cored and diced	2
3/4 cup	chopped walnuts	175 mL
2 tbsp	chopped fresh parsley	25 mL
1/2 cup	light mayonnaise	125 mL
2 tbsp	honey	25 mL
2 tbsp	cider vinegar	25 mL
1 tbsp	Dijon mustard	15 mL
1/2 tsp	celery seeds (optional)	2 mL
1/2 tsp	salt	2 mL
	Pepper to taste	

1. In a serving bowl, combine cabbage, onions, celery, apples, walnuts and parsley.

2. In another bowl, stir together mayonnaise, honey, vinegar, mustard, celery seeds, if using, salt and pepper.

3. Pour over cabbage mixture; toss to coat well. Refrigerate until ready to serve.

Bean Salad with Mustard-Dill Dressing

Serves 6

Bean salad is another staple we've grown up with over the years. Originally this salad used canned string beans, but fresh beans give it a new lease on taste, as does the addition of fiber-packed chickpeas.

TIP

Instead of chickpeas, you can try canned mixed beans. This includes a combination of chickpeas, red and white kidney beans and black-eyed peas. It's available in supermarkets.

VARIATION

French Salad Dressing

In a bowl, stir together 2 tbsp (25 mL) red wine vinegar and 1 1/2 tsp (7 mL) Dijon mustard. Add 1/3 cup (75 mL) olive oil (or use part vegetable oil), 1 minced clove garlic and 1 tsp (5 mL) dried fine herbs. Season with a pinch of granulated sugar, salt and pepper to taste. Store in covered jar in the refrigerator.

Makes 1/2 cup (125 mL).

1 lb	green beans	500 g
1	can (19 oz [540 mL]) chickpeas, rinsed and drained	1
1/3 cup	chopped red onions	75 mL
2 tbsp	finely chopped fresh dill	25 mL
2 tbsp	olive oil	25 mL
2 tbsp	red wine vinegar	25 mL
1 tbsp	Dijon mustard	15 mL
1 tbsp	granulated sugar	15 mL
1/4 tsp	salt	1 mL
1/4 tsp	pepper	1 mL

1. Trim ends of beans; cut into 1-inch (2.5 cm) lengths. In a large pot of boiling salted water, cook beans for 3 to 5 minutes (count from time water returns to boil) or until tender-crisp. Drain; rinse under cold water to chill. Drain well.

2. In a serving bowl, combine green beans, chickpeas, onions and dill.

3. In a small bowl, whisk together oil, vinegar, mustard, sugar, salt and pepper until smooth.

4. Pour over beans and toss well. Refrigerate until serving time.

Italian Pasta Salad

Serves 6

Pasta salads are always a hit. They brighten up a buffet, backyard barbecue or your dinner table. Served with HERBED GARLIC BREAD (see recipe, facing page), this salad is a meal in itself.

TIP

You can also add 8 oz (125 g) pepperoni, salami or ham, cut into thin 1-inch (2.5 cm) strips.

◆

Dried basil and oregano can be replaced with 1 tbsp (15 mL) each chopped fresh. (As a general rule, when substituting fresh for dried herbs use 3 times the amount of fresh for the dried.)

Salad:

8 oz	pasta such as fusilli *or* penne	250 g
4 oz	Provolone cheese, cut into small cubes	125 g
1 cup	cherry tomatoes, halved or quartered, if large	250 mL
1/3 cup	diced red onions	75 mL
Half	large sweet red pepper, cut into thin 1 1/2-inch (4 cm) strips	Half
Half	large sweet green pepper, cut into thin 1 1/2-inch (4 cm) strips	Half
1/3 cup	Kalamata olives (optional)	75 mL
1/3 cup	finely chopped fresh parsley	75 mL

Dressing:

1/4 cup	olive oil	50 mL
2 tbsp	red wine vinegar	25 mL
1 tbsp	Dijon mustard	15 mL
1	large clove garlic, minced	1
1 tsp	dried basil	5 mL
1 tsp	dried oregano	5 mL
1/2 tsp	salt	2 mL
1/4 tsp	pepper	1 mL

1. Cook pasta in a large pot of boiling salted water until tender but still firm. Drain; rinse under cold water and drain well.

2. In a large serving bowl, combine pasta, cheese cubes, tomatoes, onions, peppers, olives and parsley.

3. In a bowl combine oil, vinegar, mustard, garlic, basil, oregano, salt and pepper.

4. Pour dressing over pasta mixture; toss until well-coated. Let stand at room temperature for up to 30 minutes, allowing flavors to blend. Refrigerate if making ahead.

Makes 2/3 cup (150 mL)

HERBED GARLIC BREAD
Preheat oven to 350° F (180° C)

1/2 cup	butter, softened	125 mL
2	cloves garlic, minced	2
1/3 cup	freshly grated Parmesan cheese	75 mL
2 tbsp	finely chopped fresh parsley	25 mL
1/4 tsp	dried basil	1 mL
1/4 tsp	dried oregano	1 mL
2 tsp	fresh lemon juice	10 mL
1	large loaf French or Italian bread, cut into thick 3/4-inch (2 cm) slices	1

1. In a bowl cream together butter, garlic, Parmesan, parsley, basil, oregano and lemon juice.

2. Spread butter mixture on one side of bread slices; reassemble into loaf shape and wrap loaf tightly in foil.

3. Bake in preheated oven for 20 minutes or until heated through.

Best-Ever Potato Salad

Serves 6

If anything signals the arrival of summer days and backyard barbecues, it's a trusty potato salad. My version goes beyond tossing potatoes with mayonnaise. In this recipe, warm potatoes are steeped in a tasty marinade before mayonnaise is introduced. The result? A summertime family favorite.

TIP

You can also add 3 chopped hard-cooked eggs and 3/4 cup (175 mL) frozen peas, rinsed under hot water and drained well.

◆

To hard-cook eggs: Pierce the wide end of egg with a pin or egg piercer. Place in saucepan and cover with cold water by 1 inch (2.5 cm). Bring to full rapid boil over high heat; remove from heat, cover and let stand for 15 minutes. Drain and run under cold water; crack shells while eggs are still warm so they peel easily.

2 lbs	new potatoes (about 6)	1 kg
2 tbsp	red wine vinegar	25 mL
1 tbsp	Dijon mustard	15 mL
1	clove garlic, minced	1
4	green onions, chopped	4
2	stalks celery, diced	2
1/4 cup	chopped fresh parsley *or* dill	50 mL
1/2 cup	light mayonnaise	125 mL
1/4 cup	light sour cream *or* plain yogurt	50 mL
1/2 tsp	salt	2 mL
	Pepper to taste	

1. In a medium saucepan, cook whole potatoes in boiling salted water until just tender. Drain; when cool enough to handle, peel and cut into 1/2-inch (1 cm) cubes. Place in a serving bowl.

2. In a small bowl, stir together vinegar, mustard and garlic; pour over warm potatoes and toss gently. Let cool to room temperature. Stir in onions, celery and parsley.

3. In a bowl combine mayonnaise, sour cream, salt and pepper. Fold into potato mixture until evenly coated. Refrigerate until serving time.

Tabbouleh
(Bulgur and Parsley Salad)

Serves 8

The Lebanese salad tabbouleh, made with nutty-tasting bulgur, is a good example of the vibrant comfort foods from the Mediterranean that have become so popular in recent years. This refreshing green salad is often displayed next to traditional favorites like potato salad and cole slaw in the deli section of supermarkets. But you'll find it very inexpensive and easy to make in your home kitchen.

Bulgur is precooked cracked wheat that has been dried; it needs only to be soaked in water before using. You'll find it in bulk food stores.

◆

This salad keeps well for several days. It's better to add the tomatoes as a garnish just before serving to prevent the salad from becoming soggy.

3/4 cup	fine bulgur	175 mL
2 cups	finely chopped fresh parsley, (preferably flat leaf)	500 mL
4	green onions, finely chopped	4
1/4 cup	finely chopped fresh mint *or* 2 tbsp (25 mL) dried, crumbled (optional)	50 mL
1/4 cup	olive oil	50 mL
1/4 cup	fresh lemon juice	50 mL
1 tsp	salt	5 mL
1/2 tsp	paprika	2 mL
1/4 tsp	pepper	1 mL
2	tomatoes, seeded and diced	2

1. Place bulgur in a bowl; add cold water to cover. Let stand for 30 minutes. Drain in a fine sieve. Using the back of a spoon, or with your hands, squeeze out as much water as possible.

2. In a serving bowl, combine softened bulgur, parsley, onions and mint, if using.

3. In a small bowl, stir together oil, lemon juice, salt, paprika and pepper. Pour over bulgur mixture; toss well. Cover and refrigerate until serving time. Just before serving, sprinkle with tomatoes.

MUFFINS, COOKIES AND BREADS

Double Chocolate Chunk Cookies

Makes 3 1/2 dozen cookies

Flecked with white chocolate chunks and walnuts, these fudgy cookies are a favorite with my family. Served with a cold glass of milk, they're pure heaven. I'm never short of taste testers when the first warm batch comes from the oven.

TIP

For perfectly baked cookies, place baking sheet on middle rack of oven; do only one sheet at time. Wipe baking sheets with paper towels or a damp cloth to remove grease. Also let sheets cool completely before using again to prevent dough from melting and spreading out too much during baking.

◆

I like to double the recipe, bake half and freeze the remaining dough to bake another time.

◆

Nothing ruins a cookie (or any other home-baked goods) more than rancid nuts, particularly walnuts. Taste before purchasing, if possible, to make sure nuts are fresh. Store them in a covered container in the fridge or freezer.

VARIATION

Classic Chocolate Chip Cookies

Omit cocoa powder; increase all-purpose flour to 1 3/4 cups (425 mL). Replace white chocolate chunks with semi-sweet chocolate chips.

Preheat oven to 350° F (180° C)

3/4 cup	butter, softened	175 mL
3/4 cup	granulated sugar	175 mL
1/2 cup	packed brown sugar	125 mL
2	large eggs	2
2 tsp	vanilla	10 mL
1 1/2 cups	all-purpose flour	375 mL
1/2 cup	cocoa powder	125 mL
1/2 tsp	baking soda	2 mL
1/2 tsp	salt	2 mL
1 1/2 cups	white chocolate chunks	375 mL
1 cup	chopped walnuts *or* pecans	250 mL

1. In a large bowl, using an electric mixer, cream butter with granulated and brown sugars until fluffy; beat in eggs and vanilla until smooth.

2. In a separate bowl, sift together flour, cocoa powder, baking soda and salt. Beat into creamed mixture until combined; stir in white chocolate chunks and walnuts.

3. Drop tablespoonfuls (15 mL) of dough 2 inches (5 cm) apart on ungreased baking sheets.

4. Bake in preheated oven for 10 to 12 minutes or until edges are firm. (Bake for the shorter time if you prefer cookies with a soft chewy center.) Cool 2 minutes on baking sheets; remove to wire rack and cool completely.

Carrot-Raisin Muffins

Makes 16 large muffins

Packed with nuts, fruits and carrots, these scrumptious muffins are perfect for breakfast. But they are just as tasty for afternoon snacks or stowed away in a lunch box.

TIP
Have only 1 muffin pan? Place muffin paper liners in 6-oz (175 mL) glass custard cups or small ramekins and fill with extra batter. Place in oven and bake alongside muffin pan.

Preheat oven to 375° F (190° C) oven

2 cups	all-purpose flour	500 mL
3/4 cup	granulated sugar	175 mL
1 1/2 tsp	cinnamon	7 mL
1 tsp	baking powder	5 mL
1 tsp	baking soda	5 mL
1/2 tsp	ground nutmeg	2 mL
1/2 tsp	salt	2 mL
1 1/2 cups	grated carrots (about 3 medium)	375 mL
1 cup	grated peeled apples	250 mL
1/2 cup	raisins	125 mL
1/2 cup	shredded sweetened coconut	125 mL
1/2 cup	chopped walnuts (optional)	125 mL
2	large eggs	2
2/3 cup	plain yogurt	150 mL
1/3 cup	vegetable oil	75 mL

1. In a large bowl, stir together flour, sugar, cinnamon, baking powder, baking soda, nutmeg and salt. Stir in carrots, apples, raisins, coconut and walnuts.

2. In a separate bowl, beat eggs; add yogurt and oil. Stir into flour mixture just until combined. (Batter will be very thick.)

3. Spoon batter into well-greased or paper-lined muffins cups filling almost to the top.

4. Bake in preheated oven for 25 to 30 minutes or until tops spring back when lightly touched. Let cool in pans for 5 minutes; transfer muffins to a rack and cool.

Blueberry Cornmeal Muffins

Makes 12 muffins

When it comes to celebrating the pleasure of summer fruits, nothing beats juicy blueberries. They are especially welcome when teamed with lemon in these deliciously moist muffins.

TIP

To minimize the problem of frozen blueberries tinting the batter blue, place berries in a sieve and quickly rinse under cold water to get rid of any ice crystals. Blot dry with paper towels. Place berries in a bowl and toss with 2 tbsp (25 mL) of the muffin flour mixture. Use immediately; fold into batter with a few quick strokes.

Preheat oven to 400° F (200° C)

1 1/2 cups	all-purpose flour	375 mL
1/3 cup	cornmeal	75 mL
1/2 cup	granulated sugar	125 mL
2 1/2 tsp	baking powder	12 mL
1/4 tsp	salt	1 mL
1	large egg	1
3/4 cup	milk	175 mL
1/4 cup	butter, melted	50 mL
1 tsp	grated lemon rind	5 mL
1 cup	fresh or frozen blueberries	250 mL

1. In a bowl stir together flour, cornmeal, sugar, baking powder and salt.

2. In a separate bowl, beat egg; stir in milk, melted butter and lemon rind. Combine with dry ingredients until just mixed. Gently fold in blueberries.

3. Spoon into greased or paper-lined muffin cups so they are three-quarters full. Bake in preheated oven for 20 to 24 minutes or until top is firm to the touch and lightly browned. Remove from pans and let muffins cool on rack.

Bran Muffins

Makes 12 muffins

Bran muffins are never out of style. Nicely moistened with molasses, these muffins will become a morning favorite.

Preheat oven to 400° F (200° C)

2	large eggs	2
1 cup	buttermilk	250 mL
1/3 cup	packed brown sugar	75 mL
1/4 cup	vegetable oil	50 mL
1/4 cup	molasses	50 mL
1 1/4 cups	whole-wheat flour	300 mL
1 cup	natural bran	250 mL
1 tsp	baking soda	5 mL
1/2 tsp	baking powder	2 mL
1/4 tsp	salt	1 mL
1/2 cup	raisins *or* chopped apricots	125 mL

1. In a bowl, beat eggs; add buttermilk, brown sugar, oil and molasses.

2. In a separate bowl, combine flour, bran, baking soda, baking powder and salt. Stir into liquid ingredients to make a smooth batter; fold in raisins.

3. Spoon into greased or paper-lined muffin cups so they are three-quarters full. Bake in preheated oven for 20 to 24 minutes or until tops spring back when lightly touched. Let cool 10 minutes; remove from pan and cool on racks.

Gingersnaps

Makes about 5 dozen cookies

A favorite since my university days, these spice cookies would provide fuel for cram sessions before exams. Now, continuing the tradition, I bake a batch when my kids have to hit the books.

TIP

Be sure to use fresh baking soda as it makes these cookies crisp and light. Like baking powder, an open box of baking soda has a shelf life of only 6 months, so make sure to replenish both regularly. As a reminder, write the date when they need to be replaced on the container.

Preheat oven to 350° F (180° C)
Baking sheet(s), lightly greased

1/2 cup	shortening, softened	125 mL
1/2 cup	butter, softened	125 mL
3/4 cup	packed brown sugar	175 mL
1/4 cup	molasses	50 mL
1	large egg, beaten	1
2 1/4 cups	all-purpose flour	550 mL
1 1/2 tsp	baking soda	7 mL
1 1/2 tsp	ground ginger	7 mL
1 tsp	ground cinnamon	5 mL
1 tsp	ground cloves	5 mL
1/4 tsp	salt	1 mL
	Granulated sugar	

1. In a large bowl, cream shortening and butter with sugar until light and fluffy; beat in molasses and egg until creamy.

2. In another bowl, sift together flour, baking soda, ginger, cinnamon, ground cloves and salt. Stir into creamed mixture to make a soft dough. Refrigerate for 1 hour or until firm.

3. Shape dough into 1-inch (2.5 cm) balls; roll in bowl of granulated sugar. Arrange 2 inches (5 cm) apart on prepared baking sheets. Flatten to 1/4 inch (5 mm) thickness using bottom of large glass dipped in sugar.

4. Bake in preheated oven for 12 to 14 minutes or until golden. Cool 2 minutes on baking sheets; transfer to rack and let cool.

Banana Nut Bread

Makes 1 loaf

Everyone has a recipe for banana bread in their files. I've included my best. It's a simple bread that just relies on the flavor of banana and walnuts. Honey gives extra moistness that keeps it fresh for days — if it lasts that long.

TIP

Lining the bottom of baking pan with waxed or parchment paper ensures you'll never have trouble removing the bread from the pan.

◆

Left with ripe bananas on your counter but have no time to bake a bread? Simply freeze whole bananas with the peel, then leave at room temperature to defrost. Or, peel and mash bananas; pack into containers and freeze for up to 2 months. Defrost at room temperature. Frozen banana purée may darken slightly but will not affect the delicious baked results.

Preheat oven to 325° F (160° C)
9- by 5-inch (2 L) loaf pan, greased

1 3/4 cups	all-purpose flour	425 mL
1 tsp	baking soda	5 mL
1/2 tsp	salt	2 mL
2	large eggs	2
1 cup	mashed bananas (about 3 ripe)	250 mL
1/3 cup	vegetable oil	75 mL
1/2 cup	honey	125 mL
1/3 cup	packed brown sugar	75 mL
1/2 cup	chopped walnuts	125 mL

1. In a bowl sift together flour, baking soda and salt.

2. In a separate bowl, beat the eggs. Stir in bananas, oil honey and brown sugar; stir until smooth.

3. Stir dry ingredients into banana mixture until combined. Fold in walnuts.

4. Pour batter in prepared loaf pan. Bake in preheated oven for 1 1/4 hours or until cake tester inserted in center comes out clean. Let pan cool on rack for 15 minutes. Run knife around edge; turn out loaf and let cool on rack.

Oven French Toast

Serves 4

Expecting company and want to get a head start on the cooking? Here's a great breakfast dish that can be done a day ahead or frozen. When ready to serve, arrange the toasts on greased baking sheets and pop in the oven while you make the coffee.

TIP

Freeze unbaked slices in a single layer on a baking sheet lined with plastic wrap; when frozen, transfer to plastic storage bags and freeze. No need to defrost before baking; bake as directed in recipe, increasing baking time by about 5 minutes.

◆

Buy bread that is 4 inches (10 cm) in diameter or increase slices to 10 if slightly smaller.

VARIATION

Fruit Kabobs

Add colorful fruit kabobs to dress up the breakfast plate. Thread assorted fresh fruit chunks — such as apple, banana, strawberries, kiwi, pear and pineapple — onto 4-inch (10 cm) small bamboo skewers. (Trim or cut skewers in half, if necessary, to get the right length.)

Preheat oven to 425° F (220° C)
13- by 9-inch (3 L) baking dish

4	large eggs	4
1 cup	milk	250 mL
1 tbsp	granulated sugar	15 mL
1 tsp	vanilla	5 mL
8	slices day-old French bread, cut 3/4 inch (2 cm) thick	8
1/4 cup	melted butter	50 mL
2 tbsp	granulated sugar	25 mL
3/4 tsp	cinnamon	4 mL

1. In a bowl whisk together eggs, milk, 1 tbsp (15 mL) granulated sugar and vanilla. Arrange bread slices in a single layer in baking dish. Pour egg mixture over. Turn slices over and let stand until egg mixture is absorbed. Cover and refrigerate until ready to bake. (Recipe can be prepared up to this point the night before.)

2. Brush baking sheet with some of the melted butter. Arrange toasts in a single layer on sheet and brush tops with melted butter.

3. Bake in preheated oven for 10 minutes. Turn slices over; brush tops with remaining melted butter. Bake 8 minutes longer or until puffed and golden.

4. In a shallow bowl, combine 2 tbsp (25 mL) granulated sugar and cinnamon. Dip baked slices in sugar mixture and lightly coat on both sides. Serve with maple syrup and, if desired, accompany with fruit kabobs (see Variation, at left).

Peanutty Cereal Snacking Bars

Makes 24 bars

Peanut butter fans will love these no-bake bars. They're a breeze to make and taste so much better than expensive packaged snack bars sold in supermarkets. They are a nice change of pace from that other popular snack for kids — Rice Krispie squares.

TIP

Wrap bars individually in plastic wrap and freeze.Then, when making school lunches, just pop a pre-wrapped bar into each lunch bag.

13- by 9-inch (3 L) baking pan, greased

1 cup	smooth or chunky peanut butter (regular or light)	250 mL
2/3 cup	honey *or* golden corn syrup	150 mL
4 cups	toasted rice cereal	1 L
2 cups	muesli-type cereal with fruit and nuts	500 mL

1. In a large saucepan, combine peanut butter and honey; cook over medium heat, stirring constantly, until smooth. (Or place in large glass bowl and microwave at High for 2 minutes, or until smooth, stirring once.)

2. Fold in cereal until evenly coated. Press firmly into prepared baking pan. Let cool; cut into 3- by 1 1/2-inch (8 by 4 cm) bars.

Pumpkin Spice Bread

Makes 2 loaves

Love the taste of pumpkin pie, but don't have time to bake it? This appealing spice bread delivers the same intense flavor without the hassle of pie-making.

TIP

Convenient canned pumpkin is called for in this quick-to-assemble bread, but you can substitute any other kind of cooked squash, such as acorn, butternut or Hubbard sweet small pumpkins.

♦

If using fresh squash or pumpkin, cut into large pieces and remove the seeds. Place in a large casserole dish and add 1 cup (250 mL) water. Bake, covered, in 350° F (180° C) oven for about 1 1/2 hours or until very tender. Let cool. Scoop out pulp and purée in food processor. To get a thick purée like canned pumpkin, place squash in a fine-meshed sieve set over a bowl for about 2 hours to drain excess moisture.

Preheat oven to 350° F (180° C)
Two 9- by 5-inch (2 L) loaf pans, greased

3 cups	all-purpose flour	750 mL
2 tsp	baking powder	10 mL
1 tsp	baking soda	5 mL
1 tsp	salt	5 mL
1 1/2 tsp	cinnamon	7 mL
1/2 tsp	ground ginger	2 mL
1/2 tsp	allspice	2 mL
1/2 tsp	ground cloves	2 mL
3	large eggs	3
1 1/2 cups	packed brown sugar	375 mL
1 1/2 cups	canned pumpkin	375 mL
1/2 cup	vegetable oil	125 mL
1/2 cup	orange juice	125 mL
3/4 cup	raisins	175 mL

Topping:

2 tbsp	granulated sugar	25 mL
1 tsp	grated orange rind	5 mL

1. In a large mixing bowl, sift together flour, baking powder, soda, salt, cinnamon, ginger, allspice and ground cloves. Stir well with a whisk to ensure leaveners and spices are evenly distributed.

2. In a separate bowl, beat together eggs, brown sugar, pumpkin, oil and orange juice. Stir in flour mixture until batter is just combined. Fold in raisins. Divide batter between 2 prepared loaf pans.

3. In a small bowl, combine sugar and orange rind. Sprinkle over loaves.

4. Bake in preheated oven 55 to 60 minutes or until cake tester inserted in center comes out clean. Let cool on racks for 15 minutes. Remove loaves and let cool completely.

Fudgy Chocolate Brownies

Makes 24 bars

So moist and chewy, these brownies will disappear in no time. Luckily, this recipe makes a big batch, so you can stash half in the freezer — which is certainly recommended, if you want them to last more than a day!

TIP

To make neatly-cut brownies or bars: Line sides and bottom of baking pan with foil; bake as directed and let bars cool completely in pan. Place in freezer for up to 30 minutes or until partially frozen. Lift out entire batch and, using a sharp knife, cut into bars or squares. Arrange in cookie tin or rigid container with waxed paper separating the layers and freeze. Brownies, like most other bars and cookies, freeze well.

Preheat oven to 350° F (180° C)
13- by 9-inch (3.5 L) baking pan, greased

1 cup	butter, softened	250 mL
1 1/2 cups	granulated sugar	375 mL
4	large eggs	4
2 tsp	vanilla	10 mL
1 cup	all-purpose flour	250 mL
1 cup	cocoa powder	250 mL
3/4 tsp	baking powder	4 mL
1/2 tsp	salt	2 mL
1 cup	walnuts, chopped	250 mL

Frosting:

1 cup	icing sugar	250 mL
1/3 cup	cocoa powder	75 mL
2 tbsp	butter, softened	25 mL
2 tbsp	milk	25 mL

1. In a bowl, using an electric mixer, cream butter with sugar until light and fluffy. Beat in eggs, one at a time, until incorporated; add vanilla.

2. In a separate bowl, sift together flour, cocoa powder, baking powder and salt. Beat into butter mixture to make a smooth batter. Fold in walnuts.

3. Spread in prepared baking pan. Bake in preheated oven for 27 to 30 minutes or until cake tester inserted in center comes out clean. Place pan on rack to cool completely.

4. Make the frosting: In a bowl, using an electric mixer, cream icing sugar, cocoa powder, butter and milk until smooth. Spread over slightly warm brownies. When set, cut into 3- by 1 1/2-inch (8 by 4 cm) bars.

Sticky Cinnamon Buns

Makes 12 buns

Mashed potatoes are the secret ingredient that keep these sticky buns extra moist. A word of warning to the calorie-conscious: It is next to impossible to eat just one of these buns!

TIP

To make buns for morning coffee or brunch, prepare dough the day before (no need to let it rise) and place in a covered bowl in the fridge overnight. Next morning, punch down the dough and let it warm up to room temperature. A quick way to warm it is in the microwave at Low — check every few minutes and turn often. Roll out dough, spread with filling and continue with recipe as directed.

Preheat oven to 375° F (190° C)
13- by 9-inch (3.5 L) baking pan, well-buttered

1 cup	peeled potatoes, cut into 1/2-inch (1 cm) cubes	250 mL
3/4 cup	water	175 mL
1/4 cup	butter, cubed	50 mL
1 cup	milk	250 mL
3 1/4 cups	all-purpose flour (approximate)	800 mL
1/4 cup	granulated sugar	50 mL
1	pkg (2 1/4 tsp [11 mL]) quick-rise instant yeast	1
1 tsp	salt	5 mL
1/2 tsp	cinnamon	2 mL

Filling:

1/3 cup	maple syrup	75 mL
1/3 cup	butter, melted	75 mL
3/4 cup	packed brown sugar	175 mL
1/2 cup	raisins	125 mL
1/2 cup	chopped pecans	125 mL
1 1/2 tsp	cinnamon	7 mL

1. Make the dough: In a small saucepan, combine potatoes and water; simmer, covered, for 13 to 15 minutes or until very tender. Add butter; stir until melted.

2. Pour into a large mixing bowl. Using an electric mixer, beat potatoes until smooth. Add milk, 1 1/2 cups (375 mL) of the flour, sugar, yeast, salt and cinnamon. Beat for 2 minutes at medium speed until smooth. Using a wooden spoon, stir in 1 1/2 cups (375 mL) more flour to make a soft, slightly sticky dough.

3. Turn out onto floured board; knead, adding just enough flour to prevent dough from sticking, for 5 minutes or until smooth and elastic. Shape into a ball, cover with an inverted bowl and let rise for 20 minutes.

4. Prepare the filling: Combine maple syrup and 2 tbsp (25 mL) of the melted butter; pour into prepared baking pan. In a bowl combine brown sugar, raisins, pecans and cinnamon; sprinkle 3/4 cup (175 mL) over maple mixture in pan.

5. Punch down dough; roll out to 18- by 10-inch (45 by 25 cm) rectangle.

6. Brush with 2 tbsp (25 mL) melted butter; sprinkle with remaining raisin mixture leaving a 1/2-inch (1 cm) border along long sides. Roll up from one long side, pinching edges to seal. Cut dough into 12 slices and place, cut side down, in pan. Brush with remaining melted butter. Cover and let rise in warm place for 45 to 60 minutes or until doubled in bulk.

7. Bake in preheated oven for 30 to 35 minutes or until golden. Let cool on rack for 5 minutes; invert onto a large serving platter.

Fabulous Date Squares

Makes 16 squares

Here's a heritage recipe that never grows old. My version of date squares has a burst of lemon in the filling, which only enhances its traditional appeal.

Preheat oven to 350° F (180° C)
8-inch (2 L) square baking pan

Filling:

3 cups	chopped pitted dates (about 12 oz [375 g])	750 mL
1 cup	water	250 mL
1/4 cup	packed brown sugar	50 mL
1 tsp	grated lemon rind	5 mL

Crumb Layer:

1 1/2 cups	rolled oats	375 mL
1 cup	all-purpose flour	250 mL
3/4 cup	brown sugar	175 mL
1/2 tsp	baking powder	2 mL
1/4 tsp	salt	1 mL
3/4 cup	cold butter, cut into bits	175 mL

1. In a saucepan combine dates, water, 1/4 cup (50 mL) brown sugar and lemon rind. Cook, stirring, over medium heat, for 8 to 10 minutes or until dates form a smooth paste. Let cool.

2. In a mixing bowl, combine rolled oats, flour, brown sugar, baking powder and salt. Cut in butter using pastry cutter or with fingertips to make coarse crumbs.

3. Press two-thirds of crumb mixture in bottom of baking pan. Spread evenly with date filling. Sprinkle with remaining crumb mixture, pressing down lightly.

4. Bake in preheated oven for 30 minutes or until golden. Let cool on a rack; cut into squares.

Buttermilk Pancakes with Spiced Maple Apples

Makes about 18 pancakes

If I had to name one dish that brings my kids out from under their down comforters on a lazy weekend morning, this would be it. For a different twist, try these irresistible pancakes topped with spiced pear slices, too.

TIP

To keep pancakes warm, place on rack in warm oven.

◆

Extra pancakes can be wrapped and frozen, then popped in the toaster for a quick breakfast.

◆

To get a head start on a weekend breakfast, I measure out the dry ingredients for several batches of pancakes in advance, place in plastic bags and store in the cupboard. Beat in the liquid ingredients and the batter is ready for the griddle.

Spiced Maple Apples:

2 tbsp	butter	25 mL
4	apples *or* pears, peeled, cored and sliced	4
1/3 cup	maple syrup	75 mL
1/2 tsp	cinnamon	2 mL
1/2 tsp	ground ginger	2 mL
1/4 tsp	nutmeg	1 mL

Pancakes:

1 3/4 cups	all-purpose flour	425 mL
1 tbsp	granulated sugar	15 mL
2 tsp	baking powder	10 mL
1/2 tsp	baking soda	2 mL
1/2 tsp	salt	2 mL
2	large eggs	2
2 cups	buttermilk	500 mL
2 tbsp	melted butter	25 mL

1. Prepare the spiced maple apples: In a large nonstick skillet, melt butter over medium-high heat. Add apples, maple syrup, cinnamon, ginger and nutmeg; cook, stirring often, for 5 minutes or until apples are just tender. Keep warm.

2. In a bowl combine flour, sugar, baking powder, baking soda and salt. In another bowl, beat eggs; add buttermilk and melted butter. Whisk into flour mixture to make a smooth thick batter.

3. On an oiled griddle or in a large nonstick skillet over medium heat, drop 1/4-cupfuls (50 mL) of batter and spread to a 4-inch (10 cm) circle. Cook for about 1 1/2 minutes or until bubbles appear on top; turn over and cook until browned on other side. Serve with spiced maple apples.

Honey Oatmeal Bread

Makes 2 loaves

There's nothing more welcoming than the aroma of home-baked bread when you walk in the door. Who can wait to cut into a warm loaf so tasty, you don't need butter?

TIP

Bread baking know-how
For yeast to work properly, liquids must be at the correct temperature to activate the yeast. Liquids that are too hot will kill the action of yeast and dough will not rise. Cold temperatures will shock the yeast and it will not have its full leavening strength. Use a thermometer for accuracy.

Be careful not to work in too much flour when mixing and kneading, or dough will be heavy. Depending on the humidity of the flour used, you may need less or more than the amount called for in a recipe.

To measure flour correctly for all baking, give flour a quick stir, spoon into dry measure and use a knife to level the top.

Preheat oven to 375° F (190° C)
Two 9- by 5-inch (2 L) loaf pans, greased

1 1/2 cups	lukewarm water	375 mL
1	pkg (2 1/4 tsp [11 mL]) active dry yeast	1
1 tsp	granulated sugar	5 mL
1 cup	milk	250 mL
1/4 cup	dark honey (such as buckwheat) *or* molasses	50 mL
2 tbsp	butter	25 mL
2 1/2 tsp	salt	12 mL
1 cup	large flake rolled oats	250 mL
2 cups	whole wheat flour	500 mL
3 cups	all-purpose flour (approximate)	750 mL
2 tsp	melted butter	10 mL
1	egg white	1
	Additional rolled oats	

1. Place 1/2 cup (125 mL) of the lukewarm water in a glass measuring cup; sprinkle with yeast and sugar. Let stand until foamy.

2. In a saucepan combine remaining water, milk, honey, 2 tbsp (25 mL) butter and salt. Heat over medium heat, stirring, until bubbles appear around edge.

3. Place rolled oats in a large mixing bowl; pour hot mixture over. Let cool until lukewarm; if using a thermometer, temperature should read 105° to 115° F (40° to 45° C).

4. Stir in whole wheat flour and dissolved yeast; beat vigorously with a wooden spoon for 1 minute or until smooth. Stir in enough all-purpose flour to make a stiff dough that leaves the sides of the bowl.

5. Turn out onto a floured board and knead, adding just enough flour to prevent dough from sticking, for 7 to 9 minutes or until smooth and elastic.

6. Shape into a ball; place in well-buttered bowl. Turn dough to coat in butter. Cover with plastic wrap, then with clean dry towel; let rise in warm place until doubled in bulk, about 1 1/2 to 2 hours.

7. Punch down dough; knead for 1 minute to get rid of air bubbles. Divide in two. Shape into loaves and place in prepared loaf pans. Brush tops with 2 tsp (10 mL) melted butter. Cover with clean towel; let rise in a warm place for 1 1/4 hours or until almost doubled in bulk.

8. Lightly beat egg white with 1 tsp (5 mL) water; brush tops of loaves. Sprinkle each loaf with 1 tbsp (15 mL) rolled oats.

9. Bake in preheated oven for 45 minutes or until bottom of loaves when removed from pans sound hollow when tapped. Remove loaves from oven, turn out of pans and let cool on racks.

Tea-Time Scones

Makes about 12 scones

Bring out the clotted cream or the sweet butter. Set out the thick jam or fruit preserves. Brew a steaming pot of tea, invite some good friends over, then spoil them with these tender, light scones.

TIP

You can also make scones in the food processor. Process dry ingredients and cold butter using on-off turns to make crumbs. Sprinkle with dried fruits; add liquid ingredients. Process using a few on-off turns until just combined. Turn dough out onto a floured board; continue with recipe.

VARIATION

Apricot and Candied Ginger Scones

Substitute slivered dried apricots for the currants and add 2 tbsp (25 mL) finely chopped candied ginger to flour mixture.

Preheat oven to 400° F (200° C)

2 cups	all-purpose flour	500 mL
1/4 cup	granulated sugar	50 mL
1 tbsp	baking powder	15 mL
1/2 tsp	baking soda	2 mL
1/2 tsp	salt	2 mL
1/2 cup	cold butter, cut into bits	125 mL
1/2 cup	dried currants or raisins	125 mL
1	large egg	1
1/2 cup	buttermilk	125 mL

Topping:

1 tbsp	buttermilk	15 mL
2 tsp	granulated sugar	10 mL

1. In a large bowl stir together flour, sugar, baking powder, baking soda and salt. Cut in butter using a pastry blender or fork to make coarse crumbs. Stir in currants or raisins.

2. Beat egg with buttermilk; stir into dry ingredients to make a soft dough.

3. Turn out onto floured board and knead dough gently 3 to 4 times; pat or roll out using a floured rolling pin into a circular shape about 3/4 inch (2 cm) thick. Cut out rounds using a 2 1/2-inch (6 cm) floured cutter; arrange on baking sheet. Brush with 1 tbsp (15 mL) buttermilk and sprinkle with sugar.

4. Bake in preheated oven for 16 to 20 minutes or until golden. Transfer to rack.

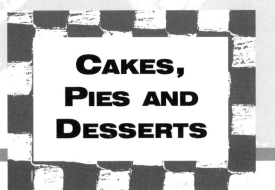

CAKES, PIES AND DESSERTS

BAKING TIPS

- Incorrect measurement is a major cause of baking failures. Use a liquid cup measure for fluids and a dry measure for dry ingredients such as flour. Spoon ingredient into dry measure and level off using a knife. Do not pack the dry measure down by tapping on the counter top; this increases the amount.

- In baking, always use large eggs, not medium or extra large, either of which can affect the baking result.

- Ingredients such as eggs and butter should be used at room temperature.

- Leave eggs on the counter for 30 minutes or place in a bowl of warm (not hot) water for 10 minutes.

- To soften butter, microwave on Defrost and check at 15-second intervals.

- Replace your supplies of baking powder and baking soda every 6 months; once opened, they oxidize and lose their leavening power.

- Replenish your spices regularly; buy the freshest dried fruits and nuts.

- For walnuts, Californian vacuum-packed walnuts are preferred.

- Always store nuts in a container in the refrigerator or freezer to keep them fresh

- For perfect cakes, loaves, bars and squares, it's essential to use the correct size of baking pan specified in each recipe.

- When a recipe calls for a baking pan, it refers to a metal pan, while a baking dish refers to glass.

- Light baking sheets, particularly the nonstick variety, are generally better than dark sheets, which attract heat and cause cookies to bake faster and/or cause the undersides to darken too quickly.

STRAWBERRY CREAM CAKE (PAGE 168) ➤

Strawberry-Rhubarb Cobbler

Serves 8

I look forward to indulging in this old-fashioned dessert when local berries and rhubarb are in season. But it's also good in winter, when I turn to my freezer for my stash of summer fruits. Serve the cobbler while still warm and top with good-quality vanilla ice cream.

TIP

If using frozen fruit, there's no need to defrost before using. If you prefer to bake the cobbler earlier in the day, reheat at 350° F (180° C) for about 15 minutes.

VARIATION

Blueberry-Peach Cobbler
Use 2 cups (500 mL) fresh or frozen blueberries and 4 cups (1 L) sliced peaches. Reduce sugar to 2/3 cup (150 mL).

Preheat oven to 400° F (200° C)
9-inch (2.5 L) round or square baking dish

4 cups	chopped fresh rhubarb	1 L
2 cups	sliced strawberries	500 mL
3/4 cup	granulated sugar	175 mL
2 tbsp	cornstarch	25 mL
1 tsp	grated orange rind	5 mL

Biscuit Topping:

1 cup	all-purpose flour	250 mL
1/4 cup	granulated sugar	50 mL
1 1/2 tsp	baking powder	7 mL
1/4 tsp	salt	1 mL
1/4 cup	cold butter, cut into bits	50 mL
1/2 cup	milk	125 mL
1 tsp	vanilla	5 mL
	Additional granulated sugar	

1. Place rhubarb and strawberries in baking dish. In a small bowl, combine 3/4 cup (175 mL) granulated sugar, cornstarch and orange rind; sprinkle over fruit and gently toss.

2. Bake in preheated oven for 20 to 25 minutes (increase to 30 minutes if using frozen fruit) until hot and bubbles appear around edges.

3. Make the topping: In a mixing bowl, combine flour, 1/4 cup (50 mL) granulated sugar, baking powder and salt. Cut in butter using a pastry blender or fork to make coarse crumbs. In a glass measure, combine milk and vanilla; stir into dry ingredients to make a soft sticky dough.

4. Using a large spoon, drop 8 separate spoonfuls of dough onto hot fruit; sprinkle with 2 tsp (10 mL) sugar.

5. Bake in preheated oven for 25 to 30 minutes or until top is golden and fruit is bubbly.

≺ BREAD PUDDING WITH CARAMELIZED PEARS (PAGE 171)

Fresh Fruit Trifle

Serves 10 to 12

A fresh twist on classic trifle, this sensational recipe stars seasonal fruits drizzled with a special orange custard cream. Traditional jam also gets replaced by tart-sweet raspberry sauce. I can count on this surprisingly light dessert to fit in well at a summer barbecue or a winter holiday meal.

TIP

Try any combination of fruits — raspberries, blueberries, sliced strawberries, halved green and red grapes, peeled kiwi slices, orange sections, apple, pear and pineapple pieces, cut into 1/2- to 3/4-inch (1 to 2 cm) cubes.

◆

Toss fruits that discolor in 1 tbsp (15 mL) lemon juice; drain before using.

◆

For a decorative top, spoon 2 tbsp (25 mL) of the raspberry sauce into a small plastic sandwich bag. Press mixture into one corner of the bag. Poke a small hole in tip of bag using a skewer and pipe mixture in a thin stream over top in a zigzag or lattice pattern.

◆

To toast almonds: Place on baking sheet in 350° F (180° C) oven for 7 to 9 minutes or until lightly toasted.

Orange Custard Cream:

1/2 cup	granulated sugar	125 mL
1 tbsp	cornstarch	15 mL
1/2 cup	orange juice	125 mL
2	egg yolks	2
4 oz	light cream cheese, cubed and softened	125 g
2 tsp	grated orange rind	10 mL
1/4 cup	orange-flavored liqueur *or* orange juice	50 mL
1 cup	whipping (35%) cream	250 mL
1	store-bought frozen pound cake (298 g), cut into 3/4-inch (2 cm) cubes	1
	RASPBERRY SAUCE (recipe follows)	
6 cups	prepared fresh fruits	1.5 L
3 tbsp	toasted sliced almonds	45 mL
	Fresh or frozen raspberries, and mint sprigs for garnish	

1. In a small saucepan, whisk together sugar, cornstarch and orange juice until smooth; beat in egg yolks. Cook over medium heat, whisking constantly, for 3 minutes until mixture comes to a full boil and thickens. Remove from heat. Beat in cream cheese, orange rind and orange-flavored liqueur until smooth.

2. Transfer custard to a bowl and cool. (Can be made 1 day ahead, covered and refrigerated.) In a bowl, using an electric mixer, whip cream until stiff peaks form. Fold into orange custard just before using.

3. Arrange half the cake cubes in bottom of a 10-cup (2.5 L) trifle or straight-sided glass serving bowl. Drizzle with half the raspberry sauce. Add half the fruit pressing an occasional piece of fruit flat against sides of the bowl. Spoon half the orange custard cream over fruit.

4. Layer with remaining cake cubes, patting down lightly. Spoon remaining raspberry sauce over and top with fruit mixture. Spread with rest of orange custard cream.

5. Cover and chill for at least 4 hours or up to 1 day ahead. Just before serving, sprinkle with toasted almonds and garnish with raspberries and mint, if desired.

	RASPBERRY SAUCE	
1	pkg (10 oz [300 g]) frozen unsweetened raspberries, defrosted	1
1/4 cup	granulated sugar	50 mL
1 1/2 tsp	cornstarch	7 mL
2 tsp	lemon juice	10 mL

1. Place raspberries in a fine sieve set over a bowl. Using a rubber spatula, press berries to extract juice and remove seeds. There should be 1 cup (250 mL).

2. Place in a saucepan; stir in sugar and cornstarch until smooth. Bring to a boil over medium heat, stirring constantly, until thickened. Remove from heat. Let cool; add lemon juice. Cover and refrigerate. The sauce can be made up to 2 days ahead.

Peach Almond Cake

Serves 8

This coffee cake is welcome at brunch, afternoon tea or dessert time. Make it year-round with other seasonal fruits such as pears, apples, pitted cherries or plums.

TIP

To peel peaches, plunge in boiling water for 30 seconds to loosen skins.

Preheat oven to 350° F (180° C)
9-inch (23 cm) springform pan or cake pan, greased

1 1/2 cups	all-purpose flour	375 mL
3/4 cup	granulated sugar	175 mL
1 1/2 tsp	baking powder	7 mL
1/2 tsp	baking soda	2 mL
1/4 tsp	salt	1 mL
2	large eggs	2
1/2 cup	plain yogurt	125 mL
1/4 cup	butter, melted	50 mL
1/2 tsp	almond extract	2 mL
3	peaches, peeled and sliced	3
3 tbsp	sliced blanched almonds	45 mL
2 tbsp	granulated sugar	25 mL
1/2 tsp	cinnamon	2 mL

1. In a mixing bowl, stir together flour, 3/4 cup (175 mL) sugar, baking powder, baking soda and salt.

2. In another bowl, beat eggs, yogurt, melted butter and almond extract until smooth. Stir into dry ingredients to make a smooth thick batter. Spread in prepared pan. Arrange peaches on top in a circular fashion.

3. In a small bowl, combine almonds, 2 tbsp (25 mL) sugar and cinnamon. Sprinkle over peaches. Bake in preheated oven for 45 to 50 minutes or until cake tester inserted in center comes out clean.

Warm Maple-Apple Pudding

Serves 6 to 8

Saucy fruit topped with a light cake batter makes one of the most soothing desserts ever created. This version hails from Quebec, where sweet and snappy Macintosh apples are paired with amber maple syrup.

TIP

Once opened, make sure to store maple syrup in the refrigerator. It also can be frozen.

Preheat oven to 350° F (180° C) oven
8-inch (2 L) square baking dish, buttered

4 cups	peeled and sliced Macintosh apples	1 L
2/3 cup	maple syrup	150 mL
1/3 cup	raisins	75 mL
1 cup	all-purpose flour	250 mL
1/4 cup	granulated sugar	50 mL
1 1/2 tsp	baking powder	7 mL
1/2 tsp	baking soda	2 mL
1/4 tsp	salt	1 mL
1/4 cup	butter, cubed	50 mL
1/2 cup	buttermilk	125 mL
1	egg	1
1 tsp	vanilla	5 mL

1. In a saucepan bring apples and maple syrup to a boil; simmer 3 minutes or until softened. Add raisins. Pour into baking dish.

2. In a bowl combine flour, sugar, baking powder, baking soda and salt. Cut in butter using pastry blender to make fine crumbs. In a bowl combine buttermilk, egg and vanilla. Pour over flour mixture; stir just until combined.

3. Drop by large spoonfuls onto warm apples slices. Bake in preheated oven for 30 minutes or until top is golden and cake tester inserted in center comes out clean. Serve warm with ice-cream, if desired.

Cinnamon Apple Crumble Pie

Serves 8

When you arrive home with your bounty of rosy apples in the fall, whip up this family treat. You won't regret it. A thick slice of warm-from-the-oven pie topped with a scoop of vanilla ice-cream is pure comfort food no one can resist.

TIP

Traditional pie pastry is made with shortening, but I prefer to make mine using butter and shortening. The reason? Not only does the buttery taste come through, but butter produces a golden crust. Another plus: the pastry is easy to handle and roll.

VARIATION

Apple Walnut Crisp

Omit pastry shell. Arrange apple filling in 9-inch (2.5 L) round or square baking dish. Prepare crumble topping: toss with 1/2 cup (125 mL) chopped walnuts or pecans. Sprinkle evenly over fruit. Bake in preheated 375° F (190° C) oven for 35 to 40 minutes or until apples are tender and topping is golden.

Preheat oven to 425° F (220° C)
Pastry for single crust 9- or 10-inch (23 or 25 cm) pie shell

Apple Filling:

8 cups	sliced and peeled tart apples, such as Macintosh	2 L
1/2 cup	granulated sugar	125 mL
2 tbsp	all-purpose flour	25 mL
1 1/2 tsp	cinnamon	7 mL
1/4 tsp	nutmeg	1 mL

Crumble Topping:

3/4 cup	large flake rolled oats	175 mL
1/2 cup	all-purpose flour	125 mL
2/3 cup	packed brown sugar	150 mL
1/2 cup	cold butter, cut into bits	125 mL

1. Roll pastry on a lightly floured surface to a 12-inch (30 cm) circle. Fit into a lightly greased deep 9-inch (23 cm) pie plate; trim pastry leaving 1/2 inch (1 cm) border. Fold under rim of dough and decoratively crimp the edges. Refrigerate.

2. In a large bowl, toss apples with sugar, flour, cinnamon and nutmeg. Spoon into prepared pie shell packing lightly.

3. Make the crumble topping: In a bowl, combine rolled oats, flour and brown sugar; cut in butter using a pastry blender or rub with your fingertips until mixture resembles coarse crumbs. Sprinkle over apples, packing lightly.

4. Bake in lower third of preheated oven for 15 minutes; reduce temperature to 350° F (180° C) and bake 40 to 45 minutes more or until apples are tender when tested with a skewer.

5. Place on rack to cool. Serve warm or at room temperature with ice-cream, if desired.

SINGLE CRUST PIE PASTRY

1 1/4 cups	all-purpose flour	300 mL
1/4 tsp	salt	1 mL
1/4 cup	cold butter	50 mL
1/4 cup	shortening	50 mL
2 to 3 tbsp	ice water (approximate)	25 to 45 mL

1. Place butter and shortening in a bowl; Freeze for 20 minutes or until firm. Cut into bits.

2. In a food processor, combine flour, salt, butter and shortening. Process to make fine crumbs. Transfer to a bowl; stir in water and gather dough into a ball. (Add just enough water to hold dough together.)

   (*Alternative method*: Place flour and salt in bowl. Using a pastry blender, cut in butter and shortening [no need to put in freezer] to make fine crumbs. Stir in water and toss; gather dough into a ball.)

3. With floured hands, flatten dough into a 5-inch (13 cm) disc. Wrap in plastic wrap; refrigerate 1 hour.

Strawberry Cream Cake

Serves 8 to 10

Nothing is more seductive than crimson strawberries, cold whipped cream and buttery-lemon cake. For me, this perfect summer dessert beats out shortcake hands down as the ultimate strawberry creation.

TIP

Strawberries can be replaced with other small fruits such as raspberries, blueberries or blackberries. Or use a combination of several berries.

◆

To make your own superfine sugar, place granulated sugar in a food processor; process until very fine.

◆

For fluffy whipped cream, make sure whipping cream is very cold before beating. As well, place the beaters and bowl in the freezer for 10 minutes before you start.

VARIATION

Raspberry Cream Cake

When fresh berries are unavailable, substitute 1 pkg (300 g) individually frozen raspberries. Do not defrost. Set aside 12 frozen berries; place in freezer and use to garnish top shortly before serving. Spread cake layers with whipped cream and frozen berries; refrigerate. Dessert can be assembled up to 4 hours ahead of serving time.

Preheat oven to 350° F (180° C)
9-inch (23 cm) springform pan, greased and floured

Sponge Cake:

3	large eggs	3
1 cup	granulated sugar	250 mL
1 1/2 cups	all-purpose flour	375 mL
2 tsp	baking powder	10 mL
1/4 tsp	salt	1 mL
3/4 cup	milk	175 mL
1/3 cup	butter, melted	75 mL
1 tsp	grated lemon rind	5 mL

Filling:

1 1/2 cups	whipping (35%) cream	375 mL
1 tsp	vanilla	5 mL
1/4 cup	superfine sugar	50 mL
3 cups	sliced strawberries	750 mL
1 cup	whole small strawberries	250 mL
	Mint sprigs	

1. In a mixing bowl, using an electric mixer at high speed, beat eggs and sugar for 3 minutes or until thick and creamy.

2. In a separate bowl, combine flour, baking powder and salt. In a glass measuring cup, combine milk, melted butter and lemon rind.

3. Beat dry ingredients into egg mixture alternately with milk mixture until batter is just smooth.

4. Pour into prepared pan. Bake in preheated oven for 35 minutes or until cake tester inserted in center comes out clean.

5. Let cake cool for 5 minutes; run knife around edge and remove sides. Place on rack to cool completely. Using a long serrated knife, slice cake horizontally to make 3 layers each about 1/2 inch (1 cm) thick.

6. In a bowl, using an electric mixer, whip cream until soft peaks form. Beat in vanilla and sugar, a spoonful (5 mL) at a time, until stiff peaks form.

7. Arrange 1 cake layer, cut side up on a large serving plate. Spread with one-third of the whipped cream; top with half the sliced berries including some juice. Arrange second cake layer on top. Spread with one-third of the whipped cream and remaining sliced berries with juice. Arrange third layer on top; spread top with remaining whipped cream. Garnish with small whole berries and mint sprigs.

Ultimate Chocolate Mousse

Serves 6

There is no more sinful and satisfying combination than rich dark chocolate and whipped cream. Serve small portions of this silky classic. It's rich. And wonderful.

Mousse can be made up to 3 days ahead. It also can be frozen; let defrost in the refrigerator for several hours or overnight.

◆

Bittersweet (not to be confused with unsweetened bitter chocolate) refers to dark European chocolate. It's recommended in this recipe for its superior flavor and can be found in supermarkets and fine bakeries. If unavailable, semi-sweet baking chocolate can be substituted.

2	large eggs	2
1/2 cup	milk	125 mL
1/3 cup	granulated sugar	75 mL
6 oz	bittersweet chocolate, finely chopped	175 g
1 tsp	vanilla	5 mL
1 1/2 cups	whipping (35%) cream	375 mL
2 oz	bittersweet chocolate, at room temperature, for garnish	60 g

1. In a metal bowl, whisk together eggs, milk and sugar until smooth. Place over a saucepan of simmering water; cook, whisking constantly (or use electric mixer), for 4 minutes or until foamy and hot to the touch. Remove bowl from heat; whisk in chopped chocolate until melted. Stir in vanilla.

2. Refrigerate for about 15 minutes, whisking every 5 minutes, until mixture cools and is slightly thickened. (Do not chill chocolate until completely set.)

3. In a separate bowl, using an electric mixer, beat cream until stiff peaks form. Whisk one-third of the whipped cream into the chocolate mixture to lighten it; gently fold in remaining whipped cream until well combined.

4. Spoon mousse into 6 stemmed wine glasses or serving dishes. Cover with plastic wrap and refrigerate 4 hours or overnight.

5. With a vegetable peeler, shave curls of chocolate onto a sheet of waxed paper; garnish mousse with chocolate curls just before serving.

Bread Pudding with Caramelized Pears

Serves 6 to 8

In the old days, bread puddings were an economy dish, simply made with stale bread and custard. But there's nothing humble about this recipe. The golden pear topping flecked with raisins transforms it into a special dessert fit for company.

TIP

Use homogenized milk to give this pudding an extra creamy texture.

◆

Can't figure out the volume of a baking dish? Look for the measurements on the bottom of dish or measure by pouring in enough water to fill completely.

Preheat oven to 350° F (180° C)
8-cup (2 L) baking dish, buttered

6	slices egg (challah) bread *or* white sandwich bread	6
2 tbsp	butter, softened	25 mL
4	large eggs	4
1/3 cup	granulated sugar	75 mL
2 tsp	vanilla	10 mL
2 cups	hot milk	500 mL

Pear Topping:

1/3 cup	granulated sugar	75 mL
2 tbsp	water	25 mL
4	pears, such as Bartlett, peeled, cored and sliced	4
1/2 tsp	nutmeg	2 mL
1/3 cup	raisins	75 mL

1. Trim crusts from bread; butter one side of each bread slice. Cut into 4 triangles each; layer in prepared baking dish, overlapping the triangles.

2. In a large bowl, whisk together eggs, sugar and vanilla. Whisk in hot milk in a stream, stirring constantly. Pour over bread.

3. In a large nonstick skillet over medium heat, cook sugar and water, stirring occasionally, until mixture turns a deep caramel color. Immediately add pears and nutmeg (be careful of spatters). Cook, stirring often, for 5 minutes or until pears are tender and sauce is smooth. Stir in raisins; spoon evenly over bread slices.

4. Place baking dish in larger shallow roasting pan or deep broiler pan; add enough boiling water to come halfway up sides of dish. Bake in preheated oven for 40 to 45 minutes or until custard is set in center. Remove from water bath; place on rack to cool. Serve either warm or at room temperature.

Creamy Rice Pudding

Serves 6

When it comes to comfort food, I put rice pudding at the top of my list. It's creamy, it's luscious and oh-so-satisfying.

If short grain rice is unavailable, use long-grain rice (not converted) instead. Long-grain rice is not as starchy so reduce the amount of milk to 4 cups (1 L) in total. Combine long-grain rice with 3 1/2 cups (875 mL) of the milk and continue with recipe as directed.

◆

Be careful of spillovers: add a walnut-sized piece of butter to rice mixture to reduce milk from foaming.

◆

Instead of using vanilla for flavoring, add a 3-inch (8 cm) strip of lemon peel to the milk-rice mixture when cooking. Remove before serving.

1/2 cup	short grain rice (such as Italian Arborio)	125 mL
5 cups	whole (homogenized) milk	1.25 L
1/3 cup	granulated sugar	75 mL
1/2 tsp	salt	2 mL
1	egg yolk	1
1/4 cup	sultana raisins	50 mL
1 tsp	vanilla	5 mL
	Cinnamon (optional)	

1. In a large saucepan, combine rice, 4 1/2 cups (1.125 L) of the milk, sugar and salt. Bring to a boil; reduce heat to medium-low and simmer, partially covered, stirring occasionally, for about 45 to 50 minutes until rice is tender and mixture has thickened.

2. Beat together remaining 1/2 cup (125 mL) milk and egg yolk; stir into rice mixture, stirring, for 1 minute or until creamy. Remove from heat. Stir in raisins and vanilla.

3. Serve either warm or at room temperature. (Pudding thickens slightly as it cools.) Sprinkle with cinnamon, if desired.

Pecan Pie

Serves 8

Intimidated by baking a pie? Don't be. This one is a breeze to bake. The filling just takes just a matter of minutes to assemble. It goes a long way to satisfy any sweet craving.

TIP

Baked pie freezes well.

VARIATION

Chocolate Pecan Pie
Line pie plate with pastry; freeze 15 minutes or until firm. Microwave 1/2 cup (125 mL) semi-sweet chocolate chips at Medium for 2 minutes or until melted. Stir until smooth; let cool slightly. Spread pastry bottom with melted chocolate; refrigerate until set. Pour in pecan filling.

Preheat oven to 375° F (190° C)
Pastry for single crust 9-inch (23 cm) pie crust
(see recipe, page 75)

2	large eggs	2
3/4 cup	packed brown sugar	175 mL
3/4 cup	golden corn syrup	175 mL
2 tbsp	butter, melted	25 mL
1 tsp	vanilla	5 mL
1 1/4 cups	whole pecans	300 mL

1. Roll pastry out on lightly floured board to a 12-inch (30 cm) circle. Fit into lightly buttered 9-inch (23 cm) pie plate or fluted tart pan with removable bottom. Trim dough leaving a 3/4-inch (2-cm) border. Fold under rim of dough and flute pastry edge. Refrigerate.

2. In a bowl beat eggs; stir in brown sugar, corn syrup, melted butter and vanilla until smooth.

3. Coarsely chop 1 cup (250 mL) of the pecans (chop nuts into 3 pieces each). Stir into filling.

4. Pour into prepared crust; sprinkle top with remaining 1/4 cup (50 mL) whole pecans. Bake in preheated oven for 35 to 40 minutes or until filling is set around edges but is slightly moist in the center. Cool pie completely on wire rack. Serve at room temperature.

Dark Chocolate Layer Cake with Rich Chocolate Frosting

Serves 8

You'll be amazed to discover that this fabulous chocolate cake is as easy to bake as a store-bought mix. It makes a very special birthday treat for friends and family.

TIP

To melt chocolate, place in a metal bowl; set over a saucepan of simmering water until melted. Or, place in glass bowl; microwave at Medium for 2 1/2 to 3 1/2 minutes. Let cool slightly.

◆

For easy clean-up, place strips of waxed paper around bottom cake layer prior to frosting. When cake is frosted, pull strips away.

◆

Frosted cake can be frozen.

Preheat oven to 350° F (180° C)
Two 9-inch (2.5 L) round cake pans, greased and floured, bottoms lined with parchment or waxed paper

Cake:

2 cups	all-purpose flour	500 mL
1 1/2 tsp	baking soda	7 mL
1/2 tsp	baking powder	2 mL
1/2 tsp	salt	2 mL
1/2 cup	butter, at room temperature	125 mL
1 1/2 cups	granulated sugar	375 mL
4 oz	unsweetened chocolate, melted	125 g
2	large eggs	2
1 1/2 cups	buttermilk	375 mL
2 tsp	vanilla	10 mL

Rich Chocolate Frosting:

1/3 cup	butter, softened	75 mL
3 oz	unsweetened chocolate, melted and cooled	90 g
3 cups	icing sugar	750 mL
1 tsp	vanilla	5 mL
1/3 cup	milk (approximate)	75 mL

1. In a bowl stir together flour, soda, baking powder and salt.

2. In another bowl, using an electric mixer, cream butter with sugar until fluffy; beat in melted chocolate,then the eggs, buttermilk and vanilla until smooth. Add flour mixture; beat to make a smooth batter.

3. Spread evenly in prepared cake pans. Bake in preheated oven for about 35 minutes or until cake tester inserted in center comes out clean. Let pans cool on wire rack for 5 minutes; run knife around edge and turn out onto wire racks to cool.

4. Make the frosting: In a bowl, using an electric mixer, beat together butter and melted chocolate until smooth. Beat in icing sugar, vanilla and enough milk to make a smooth spreadable frosting.

5. Place 1 cake layer on serving plate. Spread with frosting. Top with second layer and spread frosting over top and sides of cake.

Chocolate Swirl Cheesecake

Serves 8

The combination of chocolate swirling though thick cream cheese on top of a chocolate nut crust makes this a decadent splurge. It's hard to resist having seconds.

TIP

To prevent the top of the cheesecake from cracking, don't overbake it; it should still appear slightly underbaked in the center.

◆

Chocolate baking crumbs are available in the baking or cookie section of supermarkets.

◆

To melt chocolate, place in bowl and microwave at Medium for 2 1/2 to 3 minutes.

Preheat oven to 325° F (160° C)
9-inch (23 cm) springform pan

Crust:

1 cup	chocolate baking crumbs	250 mL
1/3 cup	chopped walnuts *or* pecans	75 mL
2 tbsp	melted butter	25 mL
2 tbsp	granulated sugar	25 mL

Filling:

1 lb	cream cheese, softened	500 g
2/3 cup	granulated sugar	150 mL
3	large eggs	3
1/2 cup	sour cream	125 mL
1 1/2 tsp	vanilla	7 mL
3 oz	semi-sweet chocolate, melted	90 g

1. In a food processor, combine crumbs, walnuts, butter and sugar. Process using on-off turns until nuts are finely chopped. Press in bottom and 1 inch (2.5 cm) up sides of springform pan. Bake in preheated oven for 10 minutes or until just set. Let cool.

2. In a large bowl, using electric mixer, beat cream cheese and sugar until smooth. Beat in eggs, one at a time until incorporated. Beat in sour cream and vanilla.

3. Transfer 1 cup (250 mL) of the batter to a bowl; stir in melted chocolate until smooth.

4. Spoon white batter into prepared pan. Top with 6 distinct spoonfuls of chocolate batter. Using a knife, cut through batter in a zigzag pattern being careful not to cut through to crust.

5. Bake in preheated oven for 30 minutes or until firm around outside and slightly moist in center. Turn off oven, leave door ajar and let cake cool in oven for 1 hour. Remove and carefully run a knife around outside edge; refrigerate.

Cranberry Cheese Torte

No longer are tart, crimson cranberries merely an accompaniment to turkey. They star in a number of dessert recipes including this crumb-topped torte.

TIP

Buy extra bags of cranberries on special and tuck into your freezer for year-round use.

◆

Cranberries freeze well for up to 1 year and can be used in any recipe calling for fresh berries. This delicious cake can be made ahead and frozen.

9-inch (23 cm) springform pan, buttered and floured

Cheese filling:

1	pkg (8 oz [250 g]) light cream cheese, softened	1
1/3 cup	granulated sugar	75 mL
1	large egg	1
1 tbsp	all-purpose flour	15 mL
1 tbsp	fresh lemon juice	15 mL
1 tsp	grated lemon rind	5 mL

Crumb topping:

3/4 cup	all-purpose flour	175 mL
1/3 cup	packed brown sugar	75 mL
1/2 tsp	cinnamon	2 mL
1/3 cup	cold butter, cut into bits	75 mL
1/3 cup	chopped pecans	75 mL

Cake batter:

2 cups	fresh or frozen cranberries, chopped	500 mL
3/4 cup	granulated sugar	175 mL
1/3 cup	butter, softened	75 mL
2	large eggs	2
1 tsp	vanilla	5 mL
1 1/4 cups	all-purpose flour	300 mL
1 1/4 tsp	baking powder	6 mL
1/4 tsp	salt	1 mL
1/3 cup	milk	75 mL

1. Make the cheese filling: In a bowl, beat cream cheese and sugar until creamy. Beat in egg, flour, lemon juice and rind until smooth.

2. Prepare the crumb topping: In a bowl combine flour, brown sugar and cinnamon. Cut in butter with a pastry blender or fork to make coarse crumbs. Stir in pecans.

3. Make the cake batter: In a bowl combine cranberries with 1/4 cup (50 mL) of the sugar; reserve. In a mixing bowl, cream butter and remaining sugar until light and fluffy. Beat in eggs and vanilla until smooth. Combine flour, baking powder and salt. Add to creamed mixture alternately with milk to make a smooth batter.

4. Spread in prepared springform pan. Sprinkle with 1 cup (250 mL) of the cranberry mixture; spoon cheese filling over. Top with remaining cranberry mixture. Sprinkle with crumb topping.

5. Bake in preheated oven for 50 to 55 minutes or until top is golden and cheese filling is set. Cool in pan on wire rack for 30 minutes before removing sides. Refrigerate until serving time.

Lemon Tiramisu

Serves 12

Worth every calorie! That's what everyone says who has sampled this luxurious variation of the Italian classic. Never since the heyday of cheesecake have we been so smitten.

TIP

This dessert can be made up to 2 days ahead.

◆

Just add the final strawberry and chocolate garnish an hour or two before serving.

13- by 9-inch (3 L) shallow baking dish

Syrup:

3/4 cup	water	175 mL
1/4 cup	granulated sugar	50 mL
1/3 cup	frozen lemonade concentrate, undiluted	75 mL

Filling:

3/4 cup	granulated sugar	175 mL
1 tbsp	cornstarch	15 mL
1/2 cup	fresh lemon juice	125 mL
1 tbsp	grated lemon rind	15 mL
2	egg yolks	2
2 cups	mascarpone cheese	500 mL
1 cup	whipping (35%) cream	250 mL
1 1/2	pkgs (7 oz [200 g] each) dry ladyfingers	1 1/2
4 oz	bittersweet or semi-sweet chocolate, grated	125 g
2 cups	strawberries, halved	500 mL
	Mint sprigs	

1. Make the syrup: In a saucepan combine water and sugar; bring to a boil over high heat; let boil for 1 minute. Remove from heat; stir in lemonade concentrate. Let cool.

2. Make the filling: In a saucepan stir together 1/2 cup (125 mL) of the sugar and cornstarch. Whisk in lemon juice and rind, and egg yolks. Cook, stirring constantly, over medium heat until thickened, about 5 minutes. Do not boil. Remove from heat; pour in bowl and cover surface with plastic wrap to prevent skin from forming. Refrigerate until lukewarm, about 25 minutes.

3. In a large mixing bowl, beat mascarpone with remaining 1/4 cup (50 mL) granulated sugar; beat in lemon curd until combined.

4. In a separate bowl, beat whipping cream with electric mixer until stiff peaks form. Using a spatula, fold whipped cream into mascarpone mixture just until no white streaks remain.

5. Using half the ladyfingers, quickly dip each in lemon syrup, then line bottom of baking dish. Spread with half the lemon cheese filling. Repeat with remaining ladyfingers and filling to form second layer.

6. Cover with plastic wrap and refrigerate at least 4 hours or up to 2 days.

7. Just before serving, sprinkle with grated chocolate; garnish with strawberry halves and sprigs of fresh mint.

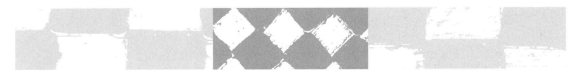

INDEX